HTML5 Geolocation

HTML5 Geolocation

Anthony T. Holdener III

O'REILLY®

Beijing · Cambridge · Farnham · Köln · Sebastopol · Tokyo

HTML5 Geolocation
by Anthony T. Holdener III

Copyright © 2011 Anthony T. Holdener, III. All rights reserved.
Printed in the United States of America.

Published by O'Reilly Media, Inc., 1005 Gravenstein Highway North, Sebastopol, CA 95472.

O'Reilly books may be purchased for educational, business, or sales promotional use. Online editions are also available for most titles (*http://my.safaribooksonline.com*). For more information, contact our corporate/institutional sales department: (800) 998-9938 or *corporate@oreilly.com*.

Editor: Simon St. Laurent	**Cover Designer:** Karen Montgomery
Proofreader: O'Reilly Production Services	**Interior Designer:** David Futato
	Illustrator: Robert Romano

Printing History:

May 2011:	First Edition.

ISBN: 978-1-449-30472-0

[LSI]

1305652947

To Kate and Tony: Remember to take the road less traveled in life, and bring along a good GPS device just in case.

Table of Contents

Preface xi

1. **Finding Our Way** 1
   Geolocation in the Past   1
       Location B.C.E.   1
       Technology with Exploration   2
       Location in the 1900s   4
   Public Availability of GPS   5
   Geolocation Now   6
   The Basics   6
   Ways to Locate   7
       Global Positioning System (GPS)   7
       IP Address   9
       GSM/CDMA Cell IDs   10
       WiFi and Bluetooth MAC Address   11
   Location and Location-Based Services (LBS)   11
   Geolocation Today   12
       Mobile Applications   13
       Augmented Reality Applications   16

2. **Geolocation: Latitude, Longitude, and More** 19
   What Are Coordinate Systems?   19
       Latitude and Longitude   20
   Geodetic Systems and Datums   23
       The Earth's Shape   23
       Common Datum   24
       Map Projections   25
   Altitude, Course, and Speed   26
       Geodetic Height   27
       Course   28
       Speed   28

    Accuracy   29

3. Geolocation API in Code **31**
    W3C Geolocation API   31
        Current API Support   32
        Other Browser Solutions   32
    The W3C Geolocation API Does More   35
    The Geolocation Object   35
    Get the User's Position   36
        PositionOptions   37
        Cached Positions   38
    Update the User's Position   38
        No Need for Polling   39
        Clearing a Watch Operation   40
    Handling a Successful Request   40
        Position Object   40
        Coordinates Object   41
    Handling an Error from the Request   43
        PositionError Object   43
    Privacy   45

4. Geolocation and Mapping APIs **47**
    A Google Maps Example   47
        The Google Maps API, Briefly   48
        Adding Geolocation to Google Maps   52
    An ArcGIS JavaScript API Example   58
        The ArcGIS JavaScript API, Briefly   59
        Adding Geolocation to Esri Maps   62

5. Saving Geographic Information **69**
    KML   70
    Shapefiles   73
        Python Shapefile Library   74
    Databases   76
        SDE   76
        PostGIS   76
        MySQL   77

6. What You Can Do with Geolocation **79**
    Geomarketing   80
        Specials and Offers   80
        Crowdsourcing   81
        Specialization   82

Geosocial   82
    Continued Growth   82
    Automatic Check-in   83
    Two Way Street of Data   84
Geotagging   85
    Digital Media and Geotagging   85
    Privacy and Geotagging   85
Geo-applications   86
    Safety/Tracking   86
    Taxi Services   86
    Search   87
    M-Commerce   87
    Other Applications   87
HTML5 and Geolocation   87
    Web Applications Supplementing LBS   88
    Web-Based LBS   95

Preface

This book explores the *W3C Geolocation API*, a specification that provides scripted access to geographical location information associated with a hosted device.* This API defines objects that can be used in JavaScript to ascertain the position of the device on which the code is executed.

 The term *geolocation* may refer to the act of identifying a person's position, or it may refer to the actual location itself.

The W3C Geolocation API brings incredible functionality to the browser. Previously, geolocation services were only made available by developers who were writing geolocation applications natively for a particular device. Now, developers have the freedom to write geolocation applications for the Web directly in the browser, and these applications have the advantage of the "write once, deploy everywhere" application model.

What Is with the Title?

Before I proceed, I would like to apologize for the title: *HTML5 Geolocation*. The Geolocation API is not technically a part of the W3C's HTML5 Specification (*http://dev.w3.org/html5/spec/Overview.html*), so calling it the *HTML5 Geolocation API* is just plain wrong and I know it.

That being said, I challenge any of you to run a Google search for "Geolocation API" or "HTML5 APIs" and see how many of the hits you get have "HTML5 Geolocation" as the title. As you will find, there are very few results besides the actual *W3C Geolocation API Working Draft*, which omits the HTML5 part. Furthermore, I attended several JavaScript sessions at the 2011 Esri Developer Summit in Palm Springs, California, and every presenter speaking about the Geolocation API also used HTML5 in conjunction with it. Every single one. These people know their Geographic Information

* *Geolocation API Specification: W3C Candidate Recommendation 07 September 2010.* Editor, Andrei Popescu, Google, Inc. *http://www.w3.org/TR/geolocation-API/*.

Systems (GIS). They live and breathe it, and they happen to work for the leading GIS software company in the world.

The simple fact is that we associate HTML5 and Geolocation. So to avoid any confusion that might have arisen had I not used HTML5, and since neither myself nor my editor could really come up with a snazzier title for this book, *HTML5 Geolocation* stuck.

Audience for This Book

This book is intended for developers interested in using the W3C Geolocation API in their web applications. The first few chapters delve into what geolocation is, its history, and how it is currently being utilized today.

These first chapters of the book are a crash course in geolocation to provide a framework for understanding what the API is about. If you are already in the GIS industry and just want to know how to implement this new Application Programming Interface (API) in your applications, or already know all there is to know about geolocation, then skip ahead to Chapter 3 to see the API in action.

Developers should be particularly interested in Chapter 3 and Chapter 4, as they discuss the API with code and examples on usage. Hopefully even nonprogrammers will be able to follow along in these chapters and gain a better understanding of what the API does. Chapter 6 ties things up by exploring what the future of geolocation holds for us all, and discusses practical applications for development using the Geolocation API.

Conventions Used in This Book

The following typographical conventions are used in this book:

Italic
> Indicates new terms, URLs, email addresses, filenames, and file extensions.

`Constant width`
> Used for program listings, as well as within paragraphs to refer to program elements such as variable or function names, databases, data types, environment variables, statements, and keywords.

`Constant width bold`
> Shows commands or other text that should be typed literally by the user.

`Constant width italic`
> Shows text that should be replaced with user-supplied values or by values determined by context.

This icon signifies a tip, suggestion, or general note.

 This icon indicates a warning or caution.

Using Code Examples

This book is here to help you get your job done. In general, you may use the code in this book in your programs and documentation. You do not need to contact us for permission unless you're reproducing a significant portion of the code. For example, writing a program that uses several chunks of code from this book does not require permission. Selling or distributing a CD-ROM of examples from O'Reilly books does require permission. Answering a question by citing this book and quoting example code does not require permission. Incorporating a significant amount of example code from this book into your product's documentation does require permission.

We appreciate, but do not require, attribution. An attribution usually includes the title, author, publisher, and ISBN. For example: "*HTML5 Geolocation* by Anthony T. Holdener III (O'Reilly). Copyright 2011 Anthony T. Holdener, III, 978-1-449-30472-0."

If you feel your use of code examples falls outside fair use or the permission given above, feel free to contact us at *permissions@oreilly.com*.

Safari® Books Online

 Safari® Books Online is an on-demand digital library that lets you easily search over 7,500 technology and creative reference books and videos to find the answers you need quickly.

With a subscription, you can read any page and watch any video from our library online. Read books on your cell phone and mobile devices. Access new titles before they are available for print, and get exclusive access to manuscripts in development and post feedback for the authors. Copy and paste code samples, organize your favorites, download chapters, bookmark key sections, create notes, print out pages, and benefit from tons of other time-saving features.

O'Reilly Media has uploaded this book to the Safari® Books Online service. To have full digital access to this book and others on similar topics from O'Reilly and other publishers, sign up for free at *http://my.safaribooksonline.com*.

How to Contact Us

Please address comments and questions concerning this book to the publisher:

O'Reilly Media, Inc.
1005 Gravenstein Highway North
Sebastopol, CA 95472
800-998-9938 (in the United States or Canada)
707-829-0515 (international or local)
707-829-0104 (fax)

We have a web page for this book, where we list errata, examples, and any additional information. You can access this page at:

http://www.oreilly.com/catalog/9781449304720

To comment or ask technical questions about this book, send email to:

bookquestions@oreilly.com

For more information about our books, courses, conferences, and news, see our website at *http://www.oreilly.com*.

Find us on Facebook: *http://facebook.com/oreilly*

Follow us on Twitter: *http://twitter.com/oreillymedia*

Watch us on YouTube: *http://www.youtube.com/oreillymedia*

Acknowledgments

First, a special thanks to my wife, Sarah, for not only taking care of things while I was busy writing (especially managing the kids), but also for putting on your editing hat and taking a red pen to the first draft of the book. I know you made this book more readable with your amazing writing skills. I am glad to have written something you were interested in reading!

I want to thank the reviewers who gave me suggestions, comments, and corrections; you made this a better book and I really appreciate it. Brian Dunn and John Jackson— thank you.

Also a big thank you to my editor, Simon St.Laurent, who not only continues to give me opportunities to write on topics I care about, but is also a great editor and a pleasure to work with. Thank you for having the confidence in me to allow me to put pen to paper once again for O'Reilly Media.

Finally, I want to thank everyone else who helped make this book happen. Thanks to O'Reilly Production Services for proofreading this work and to Adam Zaremba for all of the last minute production edits. To Karen, thank you for my cover animal. Thank you David for getting the book layout the way it needed to be. And Robert, thank you for interpreting my hand-drawn figures and creating the great illustrations that you did.

I am honored to have created a book about geolocation for the Web, and found it a pleasure to write, difficult though it was at times. I hope you enjoy it!

## CHAPTER 1

Finding Our Way

As long as people have been traveling from one place to another on Earth, they have used a variety of methods, with varying degrees of accuracy, to calculate approximately where they are located at any given time. As our technologies have improved, so has our ability to detect our position accurately. The term *geolocation* is best described as the determination of the geographic position of a person, place, or thing. In our modern era this involves the use of Internet-enabled devices (computers, routers, tablets, etc.), smartphones, or GPS-based systems.

Geolocation in the Past

While now it is easy and convenient to identify our position using devices with built-in GPS capabilities, it has not always been the case. Over the millennia people have come up with many inventive solutions to calculate where they were, which is the essence of geolocation—figuring out your real-world geographic location with available technology.

Location B.C.E.

Thousands of years ago, people relied on visual forms of geolocation to help in orienting where they were in a given area. One of the earliest forms of visual location documented in history was the *smoke signal*. Recorded evidence indicates that ancient Chinese, Greeks, and Native Americans used smoke signals to aid navigation and to communicate over great distances (as far as the eye can see). Smoke signals assisted the navigator by providing a better frame of reference to similarly shaped terrain, and would also give a rough approximation of distance from the signal. These indications would be helpful to hunting parties and other expeditions in finding their way back home.

As human cultures advanced, so did our understanding of mathematics and nature. Ancient seafarers discovered the position of the sun and stars in relation to the Earth, and calculated how to use the angles of certain "fixed" stars, like the Pole Star (otherwise known as the North Star) in their navigational calculations. Civilizations like the

Greeks, Phoenicians, Norse, Persians, and Chinese all used the stars to assist in navigating the seas, developing tools, like those discussed further later, which allowed them to venture out past the sight of land. The ability to venture farther and farther from their homes led to the discovery of new lands and the spread of their respective civilizations.

Technology with Exploration

Navigation of the oceans and seas during the Middle Ages onward was primarily for trade with other parts of the world, though exploration began to play a larger and larger role starting in the 15th century. Sailing farther distances across vast bodies of water was made possible by better tools to help in the location of ships as they moved through trackless waters.

The Arab Empire made vast contributions to navigation early in the Middle Ages while it was one of the major economic powers for over six centuries. This was accomplished in large part because of those people's ability to travel not only the river trade routes, but the oceans as well. The primary tools employed by the Arabs on their ships were a *magnetic compass* and an instrument known as a *kamal*, pictured in Figure 1-1. The kamal was a navigation device that aided in the determination of latitude. Used first by Arab sailors, this technology eventually spread to Indian and Chinese navigators as well. The kamal consisted of a rectangular piece of wood to which a string with several equally spaced knots would be attached through a hole in the middle.* The angle of the wooden card, slid along the string until aligned to a fixed star, such as the North Star, could then be measured by counting the number of knots from the end of the string to the card.

The magnetic compass used on ships during this time period used the same basic principles as a compass does today. A magnetized pointer swiveled on a pin to align itself with Earth's magnetic field. The combination of the compass and kamal allowed seafarers to calculate headings and rough latitudes in seas nearer to the equator.

As the centuries passed, the sailors of Europe began to venture farther out to sea. They had been introduced to the navigational tools of the Arab sailors, but found that the kamal, in particular, did not work very well at the higher latitudes where the Europeans sailed. For these latitudes they needed more complex devices to calculate the angles of the sun and stars. The first device developed was the *cross-staff*, also known as a *Jacob's staff* at that time. It functioned using the same basic principles as the kamal, except it was made of two longer pieces of wood shaped like a cross. It was eventually replaced by more precise instruments, namely the sea astrolabe and the quadrant.

The *astrolabe* was a graduated circle used to measure vertical angles at the sun's declination, or the declination of a fixed star. These astrolabes were built specifically for boats and meant to withstand rough seas and wind. At about this same time, navigators

---

* Launer, Donald. *Navigation Through the Ages*. Sheridan House; First American Edition, 2009.

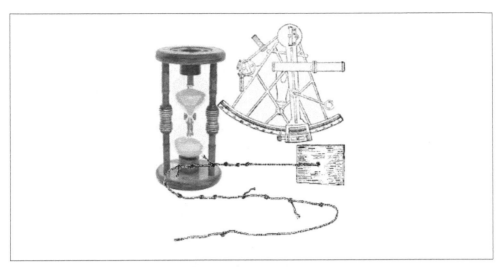

Figure 1-1. Location technology used in the age of exploration

had begun using the *quadrant* as a supplement for the astrolabe in many cases, also used to measure angles, but by measuring the projection of the shadow cast by a body like the sun. The quadrant began as a simple pole and attached arc, but evolved over time to a more complicated device with multiple poles and arcs, such as the Davis quadrant.

All of the devices to this point in history were meant to measure the latitude of a ship in the ocean, but there was no good method for calculating the longitude of the ship. Without an accurate means of calculating time and the speed at which a ship is traveling, calculating the longitude of a vessel is nearly impossible. Absent true clocks to use on their voyages, explorers began experimenting with water clocks and sand clocks—an *hourglass* was one such clock. Hourglasses were used until the accuracy of more modern watches, or *chronometers*, became available in the late 1700s.

Now able to calculate longitude with some certainty, navigators continued to search for more accurate ways to calculate a ship's latitude as it sailed the oceans. The *octant*, and finally the *sextant*, were the replacements for the quadrant and astrolabe. See Figure 1-1 for an example. A sextant measures the angle between two visible objects, and on a ship was used to measure the angle between the sun or fixed star and the horizon. To this day, the sextant is considered a viable backup navigation tool to modern GPS and radio systems as it does not require electricity.[†]

† Burch, David. *Emergency Navigation: Find Your Position and Shape Your Course at Sea Even if Your Instruments Fail*. McGraw-Hill; Maine, 2008.

Location in the 1900s

By the beginning of the 20th century, radios were used on ships to check the accuracy of the ship's chronometer and for determining direction (while also being used for communication, of course). This is accomplished by calculating a path based upon the direction that the signal was received from some source transmission, known as *Direction finding* (DF). This does not have to be a radio transmission, necessarily, as any wireless device will work as long as the object attempting DF can receive the signal. When the direction information from two or more receivers is combined, the location of the transmission can be determined through a calculation known as triangulation. *Triangulation* is the process of measuring the distance (either radial distance or directional distance) of a received signal using two or more unique transmitters. Figure 1-2 illustrates methods of triangulating a location based on both radial and directional distances. The first diagram shows a device being triangulated using the radial distance of three transmitters, while the second diagram shows a device being triangulated using the directional distance of two transmitters.

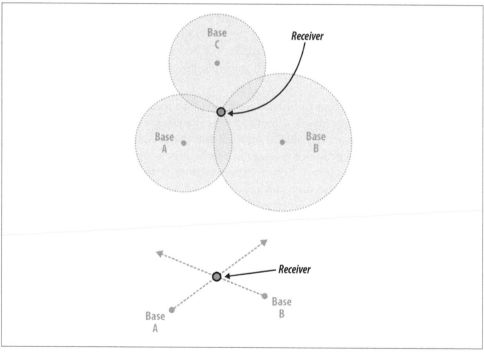

Figure 1-2. Radio tower triangulation, using both radial and directional distance triangulation techniques

In 1957 the Soviet Union launched the first man-made satellite, Sputnik, into orbit—sparking the idea of a satellite navigation system. Scientists in the United States discovered that they could monitor Sputnik's radio transmissions, and that because of the *Doppler effect*, the signal from Sputnik grew higher in frequency as the satellite got nearer to their observation posts and lower as it moved away. Using *Doppler distortion*, scientists realized they could tell exactly where the satellite was in its orbit at any given time.

 The Doppler Effect was first discovered by Austrian physicist Christian Doppler. It describes the shift in the frequency of sound waves toward and away from an observer. A good example is the sound of the sirens on an ambulance—as the ambulance approaches, the sirens get louder (compressed waves), while the siren grows steadily softer as the ambulance speeds away (stretched waves). If you could measure the rate of change of pitch, you could also estimate the ambulance's speed.‡

Over the course of the next few decades, the United States military launched a series of satellites into orbit. Some examples of these navigational satellite projects are Transit, Timation, Project 621B, and SECOR. Each project built upon lessons learned from the previous one, until the U.S. military created the Defense Navigation Satellite System (DNSS). In late 1973, DNSS was renamed Navstar. It was this system that created the basis for the GPS that we know and use today.

Public Availability of GPS

The Navstar system was originally built as a strictly military system, with no access for the civilian community. That all changed in 1983 when Korean Air Lines Flight 007 was shot down over the East Sea by the Soviet Union, killing all 269 passengers and crew. In an unfortunate set of circumstances, the flight had strayed into Soviet airspace at around the same time the Soviets had planned a missile test—claiming it was on a spy mission, Soviet interceptors shot it down. As a result, President Ronald Reagan issued a directive to the U.S. military to make the developing *Global Positioning System* (GPS) available for civilian use so that events like Flight 007 could be avoided in the future. 24 satellites would eventually be launched for this GPS array, with the first one launched in 1989 and the final one in 1994.

When it was first launched, the best quality signals were reserved for military use, while the signals that were made available to the public were intentionally degraded in what was to be known as *Selective Availability* (SA). President Bill Clinton changed this when he ordered Selective Availability to be turned off—this was done at midnight on May 1, 2000. With the removal of Selective Availability, the precision of publicly available GPS went from approximately 100 meters to 20 meters.

‡ Adrian, Eleni. The National Center for Supercomputing Applications (*http://archive.ncsa.illinois .edu/Cyberia/Bima/doppler.html*). 1995.

Geolocation Now

Since 1978, 59 GPS satellites have successfully been placed in orbit around the Earth, although as of 2010, only 30 of those satellites were still considered healthy. The United States plans to launch more GPS satellites into orbit over the next several years and has also entered into a cooperative agreement with the European Union for use of their Galileo satellite navigation system (due to be operational in 2014).

As you can see, our ability to precisely determine our location has come a long way from the days of the smoke signal. GPS has made precision possible, and is the present and future of navigational systems on Earth. Now that you have some background on how we can locate ourselves using today's technology, let us explore what geolocation is all about.

The Basics

If you picture a map of the world, your position is a single point on that map, as shown in Figure 1-3. This point is comprised of two components, *latitude* and *longitude*, that informs GPS software where you are. Once pinpointed, this information can be used by a GPS program to get more information for the user, such as nearby businesses, traffic jams, or other people. Since it has a point, the application will use a process of reverse geocoding to get this information about the area around the user.

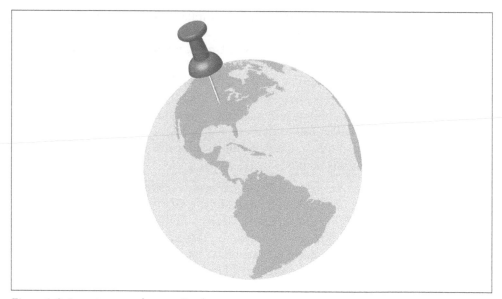

Figure 1-3. Location anywhere on Earth

Geocoding is the method of identifying the geographic coordinates associated with textual location information like street address or postal code. *Reverse geocoding* is essentially the opposite process—using associated textual location information based on a geographic coordinate.

Of course, the position does not necessarily have to come from a GPS system. The information used and how the device processes and parses location information is based upon the type of device being used.

Ways to Locate

There are many methods for modern computing devices to gain location information, and not all of them rely on GPS satellites to do so. The following is a list of many of the ways location is processed:

- Global Positioning System (GPS)
- IP Address
- GSM/CDMA Cell IDs
- WiFi and Bluetooth MAC Address
- User Input

GPS can be used on any modern mobile phones that are GPS-capable as well as on GPS-specific devices. *IP Address* location usage is also available for any device that is connected to a network or the Internet—desktops, printers, routers, etc. *GSM/CDMA Cell IDs* are used by cell phone carriers around the world. *WiFi and Bluetooth MAC Address* location usage is available on devices that use wireless technologies. *User Input* is available on any device and is software on a device requesting location, things like zip code, from the user via some input method, typically a *textbox*.

Global Positioning System (GPS)

GPS satellites continuously transmit information that GPS-enabled devices or receivers can parse, for example: the general health of the GPS array, roughly where all of the satellites are in orbit, information on the precise orbit or path of the transmitting satellite, and the time of the transmission. The receiver calculates its own position by timing the signals sent by any of the satellites in the array that are visible.

A great illustration of satellite visibility from a point on Earth can be found at *http://en.wikipedia.org/wiki/File:ConstellationGPS.gif*.

The receiver determines the time it takes to receive each message and then calculates the distance to each satellite based on this information. The distance of each satellite from the receiver, their current orbit, and the *trilateration* calculations inform the receiver of its own current position. While in radio triangulation three transmitters are enough to determine a reasonable location, there is the factor of time to be considered with orbiting satellites. It takes time, perhaps a few seconds, for a satellite signal to reach the Earth—any small clock error in a satellite, multiplied by this time, can create large positioning errors. Use of a fourth satellite removes the error from the equation (see Figure 1-4). In most cases, therefore, a receiver will use four or more satellites to calculate its position. This is not strictly necessary in cases when the receiver already has a known altitude (in the case of some fixed receivers, for example).

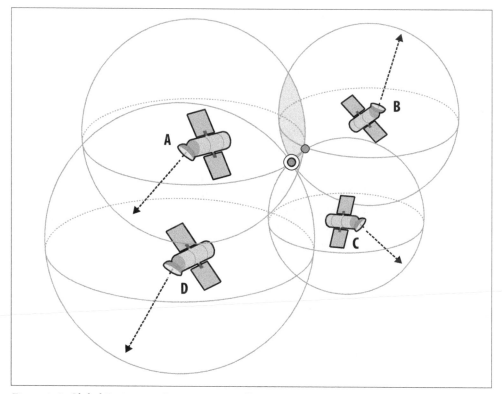

Figure 1-4. Global Positioning System using satellites

Calculating Position Using Trilateration

Trilateration is the process of measuring the distance from a point to a group of satellites to locate a position. To use trilateration, you must first know the location of the satellites you will be using. When a satellite sends a signal to a receiver, it sends (1) a time-stamp indicating when the message was sent, (2) an *ephemeris*, and (3) an *almanac*.

The ephemeris provides orbital information and clock corrections for the specific satellite. The almanac also provides data containing orbital information and clock corrections, but for the entire satellite array. The almanac data is not very precise and may be valid for up to four months while ephemeris data is very precise and valid for, at most, 30 minutes. The following steps show how to calculate a position using four satellites:

1. Take the first satellite (A) and measure its distance creating a sphere. The point is located somewhere on the surface of the sphere this measurement makes around the satellite.

2. Take the second satellite (B) and measure its distance creating a second sphere. The point is located somewhere on the perimeter of the circle created by the intersection of two spheres.

3. Take the third satellite (C) and measure its distance creating a third sphere. The point is located at one of only two points created by the intersection of three spheres.

4. Take the fourth satellite (D) and measure its distance creating a fourth sphere. The point is determined by the intersection of this fourth sphere with one of the two points.

The distance is determined using the *speed of light* as a constant, along with the time that the signal left the satellites—multiply the time by the speed of light (300,000 km/s). For accurate measurements, the satellites and clocks are accurate to the nanosecond, as all modern GPS satellites have atomic clocks built in to them.

IP Address

An *IP (Internet Protocol) Address* is a unique number assigned to any device connected to the Internet that allows it to communicate with other devices. This number may be thought of in the same way as a home address. Each of our homes has a unique address assigned to it that allows for mail to be received, take-out to be delivered, or emergency services to be directed to it. The IP address assigned to a device when it connects to the Internet allows it to send data out to other devices and receive responses back from them. Although our homes receive addresses that are more or less permanent, an IP address may be either *static* (permanent) or *dynamic* (temporary). Regardless of the type of address a device has, it will always consist of four number sets separated by periods, like this: `123.123.123.123`.

In most cases, an IP address is assigned to an Internet Service Provider (ISP) within blocks that are based on region by a local registry institution. Because of this, the country, region, and even city are generally easy to identify for a given IP address. Furthermore, with recent advances in data collected and maintained by ISPs, the device's geographical location can frequently be pinpointed to within a few meters of its actual location (see "Location and Location-Based Services (LBS)" on page 11) The biggest challenge facing someone who wants geolocation information from an IP address is that there are hundreds of these regional institutes that would need to be queried in order to gain the data—an impractical prospect.

 Though the geolocation found from a device's IP address has gotten much more accurate in recent years, it can still be misleading or off by miles. The location returned could be the location of the ISP itself, a proxy server, firewall, or any other device that passes data to the device in question, which could be physically far removed from the given position. The accuracy of the returned data will be covered in detail in Chapter 3.

Companies specializing in collecting worldwide IP address range information and consolidating it into searchable databases emerged to fill the need for quick geolocation queries. It has taken several years to accomplish, but a location identified through these companies from a device's IP address has a high level of accuracy these days. Free and pay-for-use service companies exist that provide IP address geolocation databases and APIs to access their data—IPInfoDB (*http://ipinfodb.com*), Geobytes (*http://www.geo bytes.com/*), GeoLite City/Country from MaxMind (*http://www.maxmind.com/app/ip -location*), and Quova (*http://www.quova.com/*) to name just a few. The Geolocation API gathers a position (see "Latitude and Longitude" on page 20) from a user's IP address without the developer needing to make a call to one of these databases, though as we will see, these companies provide a great deal of additional information about the user's location that the API does not expose.

GSM/CDMA Cell IDs

A *Cell ID* is the unique number that identifies each mobile device in a particular cell network, much like an IP Address identifies a device on a network. The two most popular networks available are *Global System for Mobile Communications (GSM)* and *Code Division Multiple Access (CDMA)*. The type of cell service you require is based on the area you are attempting to gain coverage in.

GSM is the oldest of the mobile service technologies, and therefore enjoys a certain robustness over other technologies available in the market. GSM is a 2G technology that is available in over 200 countries, and recent data suggests it is used by over 75% of the world's mobile users. The availability of GSM to migrate to 3G and 4G services (Evolved High Speed Packet Access (HSPA+), Long Term Evolution (LTE), and Service Architecture Evolution (SAE)) is also very straightforward, making it the standard in use by nearly four billion customers. Though GSM technologies cannot hold the same amount of data as other technologies, it does have a high quality level due to the ability to place repeaters inside and outside of buildings where reception would otherwise diminish. This makes it a good carrier with less service interruption.

CDMA is a newer technology than GSM, and comes in both 2G (cdmaOne(TM)) and 3G (CDMA2000(R) and WCDMA) types of service. The advantage of CDMA technology is that it allows many users to occupy the same time and frequency portions in a given band, something that GSM cannot do. CDMA networks, like GSM, are also migrating to LTE technologies to support the growing demand for 4G networks.

Regardless of what type of technology the mobile device is using, the basic principle of having a unique identifier on the network is what really matters. Using triangulation, the Cell ID's latitude and longitude can be identified, allowing it to be geolocated. The more towers that are used to triangulate the position of the mobile device, the more accurate the location will be. This is why geolocation that relies on this type of technology works better in urban environments—where there are more towers in closer proximity to one another—than in rural areas.

 In the United States, with the advent of Enhanced 9-1-1 (E911) services, the Federal Communications Commission (FCC) mandated that all carriers must meet a minimum of 95% of all handsets resolving their position to within 300 meters. This mandate has considerably improved the geolocation capabilities of mobile devices on cell networks.

WiFi and Bluetooth MAC Address

WiFi and Bluetooth MAC Addresses work in a similar fashion to IP addresses on a device. The Media Access Control (MAC) address is a unique number assigned to the interface, usually by the manufacturer of the interface card. This number was intended to be a permanent and globally unique identifier, however more modern hardware allows for the address to be manually changed; this is a practice known as *MAC spoofing*. A typical MAC address will look something like this: `12-34-56-78-9A-BC`.

The MAC address for a WiFi router is simply the address found on the interface for the wireless device. In the same way, the MAC address for a Bluetooth device is the address found on its interface. Using this address in a similar manner as an IP address, a latitude and longitude, and thus a physical location, can be obtained.

Location and Location-Based Services (LBS)

Your *location*, or *position*, is a point in physical space designated by the latitude and longitude that a device occupies on the Earth's surface. The surface of the Earth, however, is not flat. A location will have other information associated with it, as we will see in Chapter 2, that will help pinpoint the exact space on the surface.

Other information can also be retrieved as part of a location—information that is more readily consumable by people. This information includes country, region or state, city, postal code, street address, timezone, domain name, Internet Service Provider (ISP), language, company name, and connection speed. What information corresponds to or is available with a latitude and longitude depends on the method used to retrieve the location (GPS, IP Address, etc.).

A *location-based service* (LBS) is usually a service running on a mobile device that provides facts or recreational information. It employs geolocation to make the facts or entertainment more personal to the user of the application. An example of a typical location-based service is one that identifies the location of a device and then discovers the location of restaurants in the immediate vicinity of that location. As location-based services become more common, their commercial value will become more readily evident to corporations, who can use them to personalize users' experiences with location-aware weather, coupons, and advertising. This is already becoming more common, and will only continue to grow in the future.

A location-based service begins by gathering a location for the device using one of its available methods, which could be through GPS, the GSM/CDMA Cell ID, or its IP Address, for example. Once it has a location in latitudinal and longitudinal coordinates, it can then retrieve whatever additional information it is programmed to receive. This information is then presented to the user, most likely to be interacted with in some fashion.

Some popular examples of location-based services are:

- Turn-by-turn navigation to an inputted address
- Notifications regarding traffic congestion or accidents
- Location of nearby businesses, restaurants, or other services
- Social interaction with other people nearby
- Safety applications for tracking members of a family

This list could go on and on, as there are countless things to be done with location-based services today. Location-based services are a large part of geolocation today, but they are not the only services that use geolocation for their functionality. I encourage you to check out sites that keep tabs on the location-based services market, as it is continually growing—LBSZone.com (*http://www.lbszone.com/*) is a good place to start. Sidney Shek, writing for CSC, a company that has been developing technology solutions for more than 50 years, also wrote a great paper on Location-based services that can be found at *http://assets1.csc.com/lef/downloads/CSC_Grant_2010_Next_Generation _Location_Based_Services_for_Mobile_Devices.pdf*.

Geolocation Today

These days (by which I mean starting around 2009) geolocation has become a hot topic, especially among mobile software developers. The number of applications available for mobile devices, and smart phones in particular, increases daily. The great thing about all of this new software is that it is not focused on only one market, but instead encompasses a wide variety of uses. Many of these applications are geared towards social media and interaction, but there is also a growing number of services that offer specialized searching based on location, real-time tracking, and emergency services applications.

Mobile Applications

Mobile geolocation applications have been growing in popularity since 2004, with the development of one of the first modern social media applications: Yelp. There were other applications that came before Yelp, but this application seemed to have a broader appeal—the coming explosion of smart phones certainly helped. Since that time, there has been a huge growth in this market, from network and hardware applications direct from providers to *Software Development Kits* (SDKs) from software vendors that have led to the plethora of solutions available today. Cloud solutions are certainly gaining traction as well—Esri's collaboration with Amazon Web Services starting in February 2010 is proof of this.

Consider that every major network provider, companies like Verizon Wireless (*http://www.verizonwireless.com/*), AT&T (*http://www.wireless.att.com/*), Sprint (*http://www.sprint.com/*), T-Mobile (*http://www.t-mobile.com/*), etc., has some sort of geolocation application available on its devices when they are shipped. On top of that, the Operating Systems (OS) provided for these devices (iOS (*http://developer.apple.com/devcenter/ios/index.action*), Android (*http://developer.android.com/sdk/index.html*), RIM (*http://us.blackberry.com/developers/*), etc.) have provided SDKs to allow developers the ability to write native applications for all of these devices. This is where the real explosion in location-based services has come from, particularly in the creation of:

- Social Check-in Apps (Foursquare, Gowalla, Yelp, etc.)
- Location-sharing Apps (Shopkick, Glympse, etc.)

Social Media Applications

Yelp (*http://www.yelp.com/*), released in 2004 by Jeremy Stoppelman and Russel Simmons, was one of the first mainstream social media apps that aimed to connect local businesses with people in the community. Yelp provided a means for users to find and review businesses, and read the reviews submitted by others for any particular place. It also allowed businesses to alert users to special events and offers available. Yelp is still going strong as an application, with over 45 million people having visited Yelp in the past 30 days, as of January 2011.[§] Yelp is all about connecting a community together using geolocation at its base, and many later applications modeled aspects of their software on Yelp's core concepts.

Google Latitude (*http://www.google.com/latitude*) is a geolocation application that builds upon Google's Maps application, and allows you to see where your friends are at any time when they allow it, while also sharing your location with them. Google

§ About Us | Yelp (*http://www.yelp.com/about*).

originally purchased Dodgeball, a social networking application written by Dennis Crowley, in 2005 and shut it down in 2009 in favor of Latitude. Latitude is available for both mobile phones and desktop computers. Though more fully featured (sharing location, checking-in, home screen widget, privacy) on Android phones, the basic ability to share your location with others and see where your friends are is available on pretty much every platform around today. Latitude is Google's solution for a social media check-in application, but this just scratches the surface of social media applications available.

Not too long after Yelp was launched, Loopt (*http://www.loopt.com/*) was created by two sophomores at Stanford University, Sam Altman and Nick Sivo, who were later joined by Alok Deshpande, and Rick and Tom Pernikoff, with the sole purpose of creating a geolocation application to help users discover everything around them. Loopt, unlike Yelp, was designed with a focus on the people using the application rather than just businesses or locations, creating a more robust social media application.

In 2007, Gowalla (*http://gowalla.com/*) entered the location-based services scene and started the concept of the "check-in" at "Spots" based on your geolocation. Gowalla, co-founded by Josh Williams and Scott Raymond, aims to allow users to interact socially by sharing their travel experiences, photos, and comments, while adding a social game aspect with the ability to earn pins and rewards that you add to your "Passport." More recent releases of Gowalla now have integration with newer social location-based service applications, such as Foursquare, Facebook Places, and Twitter.

SCVNGR (*http://www.scvngr.com/*), created in 2008 by Seth Priebatsch, focuses on social-networking as a game platform. The idea behind playing SCVNGR is going out to different places, doing challenges while there, and earning points in the process. Because SCVNGR was designed as a platform and not simply an outward-facing application, organizations, educational institutions, and individuals are able to build their own challenges and integrate rewards for locations directly into the game.

Foursquare (*http://foursquare.com/*), dubbed "the breakout mobile app" of the 2009 South by Southwest Music and Media Conference (SXSW), was created by Dennis Crowley (creator of Dodgeball) and Naveen Selvadurai (see Figure 1-5). It mashes together ideas from its predecessors, being partly a game and partly a social media experience to share information with other users. With Foursquare, users "check-in" to a location; earning them points and possibly "mayorships" and badges. Users can also add tips for locations they visit, aiding others who may be trying to find a certain place themselves.

2010 was designated as the "Year of Geolocation," and rightly so. Foursquare saw enormous growth in its user-base, and at the time of this writing has over 7.5 million users, making it the most popular of all the geolocation applications available currently. Who is to say, however, what the next big application will be? The social-media giant, Facebook (*http://www.facebook.com/*), launched its own location-based service in the form of Facebook Places in 2010, and with its more than 500 million active users the

Figure 1-5. Social media apps and Geolocation go hand-in-hand

potential exists for geolocation to explode. The social media side of geolocation applications will continue to be strong for the years to come.

Location-sharing Applications

Glympse (*http://www.glympse.com/*) was founded in 2008 by three ex-Microsoft employees—Bryan Trussel, Jeremy Mercer, and Steve Miller—with a different approach for sharing location information with others. Glympse, like Google Latitude, restricts who can see a user's location to only those that the user chooses. The difference from all other geolocation applications, however, is in how the information is shared. Instead of relying on the user to check-in to various places and those updates being shared by other individuals, Glympse shows where the user is in real-time on a web-based map by using the GPS on the device on which the application is running. This sharing lasts only for a predetermined period of time, and requires no user interaction beyond starting the "glympse."

Shopkick (*http://www.shopkick.com/*) was created in 2009 by Cyriac Roeding, Jeff Sellinger, and Aaron Emigh to create a new shopping experience for people utilizing their phones. Partnering with some of the largest retailers in the United States, it provides users with the opportunity to earn rewards and special offers simply by walking into the stores. It is not necessary for the user to check in to the store when she enters, either, because Shopkick uses GPS to check the user's proximity to participating stores and automatically recognizes when she has entered (within a given error radius).

The location-sharing application market will continue to grow, as the idea of permitting others to view where you are without having to interact with the application becomes a more comfortable idea. Privacy concerns will be the main hurdle for these types of applications. The market may see more inventive geolocation solutions to these location-based services if consumers can be convinced that applications of this type will be used less for social interaction and more for service-oriented products like Shopkick.

Augmented Reality Applications

Augmented reality is a combination of a real world view (usually through a camera or other lens) and a computer-generated view superimposed with sensory input. For example, point a mobile phone's camera at a city street and the augmented reality application will display graphical and textual information about the streets, cars, people, buildings, and weather that it "sees" through the lens. All of this information would be placed in front of the actual camera pictures, giving the user vast amounts of supplemental information in real-time.

Current augmented reality applications on mobile devices use geolocation as an aid in figuring out what information should be given to a user at any given time. In addition, the mobile device would be using all of its other sensors to fill in the additional data it needs to properly display the augmented reality. The market is still new for these types of application, and though there are not many available today, I would expect to see more and more uses for such technology in the near future.

Layar (*http://www.layar.com/*), founded in 2009 by Claire Boonstra, Maarten Lens-FitzGerald, and Raimo van der Klein in Amsterdam, the Netherlands, is a mobile augmented reality platform that provides different types of information on top of the camera's displayed image. Some of the information currently available includes weather, real estate, government, restaurants, tourism, and entertainment venues. The information viewable is called *layers*, which would appear as web pages in a normal browser. In 2011, Layar was named as a Technology Pioneer by the World Economic Forum and TIME magazine.

The acrossair Augmented Reality Browser (*http://www.acrossair.com/apps_acrossair browser.htm*) is a browser built to handle searching with Google or Wikipedia, pull in pictures from sources like Flickr and Panaromia, and access social media like Twitter or Yelp—all from a single application that enhances a camera's reality. Released to the iPhone App Store in late 2009, acrossair is continually improving its application to make it as useful a navigation aid as possible. It is built to be a one-stop application for finding everything you could possibly want about a particular point of interest.

Yelp Monocle is an augmented reality service that was added to the existing Yelp social media application in 2009. Using the phone's GPS and compass, it displays markers for nearby businesses on top of the camera's view based on the direction the phone is facing, as shown in Figure 1-6. These markers grab data from the main Yelp database of businesses and display the reviewer rating, how far away each place is, type of business, and when available, whether the business is open or closed.

Figure 1-6. Yelp Monocle in action on Android

As we move farther from inception of these initial augmented reality applications, we should expect to see many more offerings in this particular market. Augmented reality is a cutting-edge technology that, combined with geolocation, has the potential to offer some truly spectacular applications very soon.

## CHAPTER 2

Geolocation: Latitude, Longitude, and More

In Chapter 1, we covered the basics of geolocation, including what geolocation means, how geolocation information is gathered from different sources depending upon the device, and some common applications that implement geolocation today. Several key terms have also been mentioned, like *latitude*, *longitude*, and *altitude*; yet no definition has actually been given for any of these terms. Perhaps you are already well-versed in the GIS vernacular, but in case you are not, this chapter is meant to give a better understanding about exactly what information the W3C Geolocation API will be giving the developer. Recognizing exactly what information you are being passed and how to manipulate it properly will allow you to build better applications, if for no other reason than so that you will not misinform the end-user about the data.

What Are Coordinate Systems?

We have discussed the location (position) for a device, found using GPS or some other location method, given in latitude and longitude. These are called the *coordinates* of the particular device. In order to locate a device on the Earth, it is given a set of numbers which represents its place on the globe. These numbers make up the system by which we can then extrapolate positions.

There are many types of coordinate systems used in mathematics and everyday life—in fact, the most basic of coordinate systems was most likely taught to you when you were first learning to add and subtract: the *number line*. Other types of coordinate systems that should be familiar to those who took other mathematics classes are the *Cartesian coordinate system* (x, y, and z) and the *polar coordinate system* (r, θ). For geolocation, it is a *geographic coordinate system* that is used. With a geographic coordinate system, coordinates are expressed in latitude, longitude, and elevation.

Latitude and Longitude

To understand how latitude and longitude works, picture a globe with lines running both horizontally and vertically at (roughly) equal spacing between them, as shown in Figure 2-1. I mention roughly because, as we will see in "The Earth's Shape" on page 23, the Earth is not a perfect sphere, and there will be small variations in the spacing of the horizontal lines. This system of latitude and longitude was probably first created in Egypt, but Eratosthenes may have been the first person to draw these lines in the third century B.C.E. It was a later Alexandrian scholar who divided up the Earth into an orderly grid using *degrees* (degree, "step").*

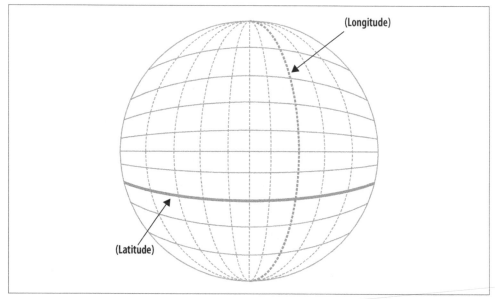

Figure 2-1. Diagram of latitude and longitude on Earth

The horizontal lines on the globe are the lines of *latitude*, and are spaced about 69 miles (111.04 kilometers) apart from one another. The degrees of latitude are numbered from "zero degrees" at the Earth's equator, to 90° in both the northern and southern hemispheres. The North Pole corresponds to 90° North, while the South Pole corresponds to 90° South. Latitude is expressed by φ, or the lower-case Greek letter *phi*.

The vertical lines on the globe are the lines of *longitude*. These lines converge at the North and South Poles, and run their widest (again, about 69 miles or 111.04 kilometers) at the equator. Lines of longitude are also known as *meridians*. The Prime Meridian, "zero degrees" longitude, was established in 1884 at Greenwich, England. From the Prime Meridian, the lines of longitude are numbered to 180° in both the eastern

---

* Garrison, Tom. *Oceanography: an invitation to marine science*. Cengage Learning, 2007.

---

and western hemispheres. Longitude is expressed by λ, or the lower-case Greek letter lambda.

 Prior to 1884, any seafaring nation could set its own "zero" longitude when it issued navigational charts. This happened quite often over the centuries. In fact, this practice dates back to that first Alexandrian scholar who selected the Egyptian city of Alexandria as the first "zero" longitude.

Decimal Degrees versus Degrees Minutes Seconds

In order to gain the necessary precision when locating a point on the Earth, the degrees of latitude and longitude are actually broken down into degrees (°), minutes ('), and seconds ("). Every minute is made up of 60 seconds, and every degree is made up of 60 minutes. An example coordinate point would be the St. Louis Arch, which can be found at 38°37'29"N, 90°11'7"W—this is 38 degrees, 37 minutes, and 29 seconds north of the equator and 90 degrees, 11 minutes, and 7 seconds west of the Prime Meridian.

When you read about coordinates that are in degrees, they will generally be found in one of these three forms:

- Degrees, minutes, and seconds (plus fractions of a second)
- Degrees and minutes (plus fractions of a minute)
- Decimal degrees

The coordinates of the Arch were of this first form, *degrees, minutes, and seconds* (DMS). The second form (degrees and minutes) is not as common, but still available to use. The third form, *decimal degrees*, converts the minutes and seconds of a DMS coordinate into a fraction of a degree. Decimal degrees differ from the other two types in that they do not indicate the direction of the latitude and longitude with cardinal directions (north, south, east, west), but instead simply display a positive or negative number. For example:

38°37'29"N	38.624722
56°12'13"S	-56.203611
124°11'7"W	-124.185278
12°57'24"E	12.956667

Conversion: DMS to Decimal Degrees

Converting from a DMS coordinate to a decimal degree coordinate is straightforward, following these steps:

1. Calculate the total number of seconds.
2. Take this total and divide it by 3,600 (the number of seconds in a degree).

3. Add this fraction to the whole number of degrees.

4. If the coordinate is a South latitude or West longitude, negate the result.

We will follow these steps to convert the longitude part of the Arch's coordinate, 90°11'7"W, to see these steps in action:

1. Calculate the total number of seconds: **11'7" = ((11 * 60) + 7) = 667**.

2. Take this total and divide it by 3,600: **(667 / 3,600) 0.185278** .

3. Add this fraction to the whole number of degrees: **90 + 0.185278 = 90.185278**.

4. It is a West longitude, so negating it gives us: **-90.185278**, as it is West of Greenwich.

Conversion: Decimal Degrees to DMS

Simple enough, right? Converting from a decimal degree coordinate to a DMS coordinate is just as straightforward, following these steps:

1. Subtract the whole degrees from the whole coordinate, leaving the fraction.

2. Multiply the fractional part by 60 (this is the number of minutes).

3. Subtract the whole minutes from the full minutes, leaving the fraction.

4. Multiply the fractional part by 60 (this is the number of seconds).

5. If the original coordinate was negative and a longitude, then keep the sign of the whole degree, or remove the sign and add a W, otherwise add an E. Likewise, if the original coordinate was negative and a latitude, then keep the sign of the whole degree, or remove the sign and add an S, otherwise add an N.

Perhaps slightly more confusing as far as directions go, but following an example should make it much clearer. Let us take -90.185278 (a longitude):

1. Subtract the whole degrees from the whole coordinate, leaving the fraction: **90.185278 – 90 = 0.185278**.

2. Multiply the fractional part by 60: **(0.185278 * 60) = 11.11668**.

3. Subtract the whole minutes from the full minutes, leaving the fraction: **11.11668 – 11 = 0.11668**.

4. Multiply the fractional part by 60: **(0.11668 * 60) = 7.0008** (drop the 0.0008 to get 7).

5. The original coordinate was negative and a longitude, so we will drop the sign and add a W: **90°11'7"W**.

If at this point you are unsure why we went through all of this, all will become clear in Chapter 3 when we look at what the W3C Geolocation API returns after a location request is made. This stuff matters, trust me!

Geodetic Systems and Datums

If everything were simple, the geographic coordinate system would be enough to describe where points fall on the Earth. Because of the Earth's irregular shape, however, things are not quite so simple and a system was needed to translate positions indicated on maps to their real positions on the Earth. This system is called a *geodetic system*. The references used in the geodetic system to translate coordinates are called *datums*—a *geodetic datum* is a reference used in surveying and geodesy.

 Geodesy is the branch of geology that studies the shape of the earth and the determination of the exact position of geographical points. Geodetic, geodesic, or geodesical refer to these measurements.[†]

Geodetic datums are used to orientate the geographic coordinate system, fix its origin, and define the shape of the Earth. For geolocation, the geodetic datums that interest us are those that model the Earth as a flat surface—it is not easy to display a three-dimensional Earth as a map, especially on the Web. To use Google as an example, going to *http://maps.google.com/* will display a map of the Earth that is modeled as a flat surface, while going to *http://earth.google.com/* shows the Earth in three-dimensions. Each of these maps uses different datums to display the same data.

The Earth's Shape

I have been making a big deal about the shape of the Earth, how it affects the geographic coordinate system and latitudes, and it being the cause for needing geodetic datums. So what gives?

We were probably all taught that the ancient Greeks, as far back as the sixth century B.C.E., had at least the rough belief that the Earth was round—a sort of Pythagorean sphere. Mathematicians and philosophers refined their theories and experiments over the centuries, coming closer and closer in approximation to the shape we know the Earth to be today. What is sometimes omitted from our curriculum, however, unless we take more advanced science classes as we get older, is that the Earth is not a true sphere.

Sure, a sphere is a close approximation to the shape of the Earth, and will work as a mapping model for many applications (including Google Earth). However, as we have discovered through advances in the study of gravitational fields and better geographic data (satellites aided greatly here), the Earth bulges around the equator and is flattened at both poles. A better definition for the shape of the Earth would be an *oblate spheroid*, as shown in Figure 2-2. Because of the elliptical shape of the Earth, datums are

---

† Princeton University "About WordNet." WordNet. Princeton University. 2010. *http://wordnet .princeton.edu/*.

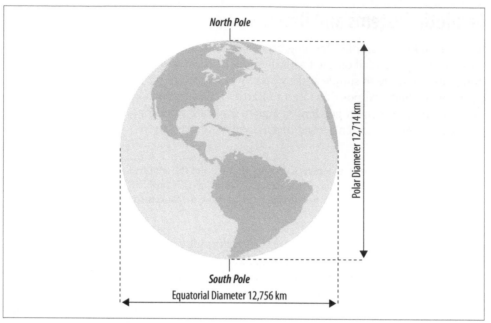

Figure 2-2. The Earth is an oblate spheroid

used to satisfy simplifying the Earth into simpler two- and three-dimensional models everyday users can consume.

Common Datum

As Mathematicians modified and recalculated their ideas of the Earth's shape and size, the datums that they used had to be modified as well. There have been many different datums over time, and these datums have evolved from ones that described the Earth as a sphere, to today's more modern datums that describe the oblate spheroid we now know the Earth most closely approximates.

Since the Earth is not a perfect spheroid, using a more localized datum will yield a better representation of that area than using a globally encompassing datum. The following are a few of the more common "global" datums in use today:

- World Geodetic System (WGS 84)
- North American Datum (NAD 83)
- European Datum (ED 50)

By contrast, the following are a sample of the many more localized datums in use around the globe:

- Ordinance Survey of Great Britain (OSGB 36)
- Swiss Datum (CH 1903)

- Japanese Datum (TOKYO)
- Pulkovo Datum (S-42)

The differences in the coordinates between any two datums is called the *datum shift*, and is an important consideration when looking at a map. The shift between datum depends on many factors, including the elevations of the datum in question. For example, while the difference between WGS 84 and NAD 83 is very small (less than 70 meters on average), the difference between WGS 84 and OSGB 36 is roughly double (around 140 meters). Considering the size of the Earth, both of these differences may seem small, but when attempting to place a coordinate in a smaller, "local" environment, 140 meters (459 feet) could mean a *few city blocks*.

WGS 84

The *World Geodetic System* is a global datum that was first created in 1960 (WGS 60) by the United States Department of Defense and scientists around the world. Several factors led to the need of a consolidated world system by which more localized datums could be referenced. Most importantly, the large geodetic datums in existence at the time (NAD 27, ED 50, etc.) were not sufficient to create a global system with sufficient accuracy. Also, there was a growing need for global maps, due to growth in global trade, growth in global tourism, and the burgeoning space science programs. World Geodetic System has seen several revisions, including WGS 66 and WGS 72. The latest revision is WGS 84, a datum that dates from 1984 and was last revised in 2004.

WGS provides three key components that are used for any geodetic measurements: a framework for placing coordinates on the Earth, a *geoid* which defines a Mathematically idealized likeness of the Earth's surface (the global mean sea level), and a reference spheroid. The reference spheroid for the WGS is, of course, an oblate spheroid over which the latitude and longitude coordinate system can be placed. WGS 84 began using a geoid based on calculations from the Earth Gravitational Model of 1996 (EGM 96) when it was revised in 2004. Prior to this, it was using EGM 84.

 It is necessary to update the geoid for a global datum occasionally, as natural physical changes in the Earth modify its gravitation and rotation. For example, based on calculations by Richard Gross of the NASA Jet Propulsion Laboratory, the M9.0 2011 Honshu earthquake raised the sea level by 0.22 meters and shifted the ocean floor enough to shorten the length of a day by 1.8 microseconds, while the M8.8 2010 Chile earthquake raised the sea level by 0.16 meters.

Map Projections

To produce a map of the Earth, either a physical map or a map displayed in a browser, it must be *projected* from its three-dimensional form to a two-dimensional representation. For smaller areas of the Earth, this is not such a big deal, but when producing a map of the entire globe, it becomes more challenging. Using a datum as a reference, a map is projected to display certain aspects of the Earth—scale, distance, area, shape, etc. No map can, unfortunately, protect every aspect and there will have to be compromises on some aspects in order to preserve others.

On the Web, all major vendors in map data (Esri, Google, Microsoft, etc.) use a map projection based on the *Mercator projection*. The Mercator projection is named after the Belgian cartographer Gerardus Mercator, who created the cylindrical map projection in 1569. With this projection, all latitudinal and longitudinal line cross at right angles (90 degrees), which keeps geographical aspects of the Earth normal near the equator, but greatly skews those near the poles, as shown in Figure 2-3—Greenland is not actually nearly the same size as Africa.

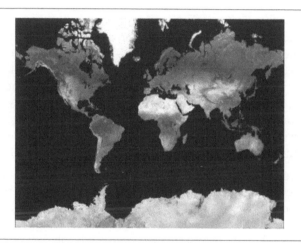

Figure 2-3. A map of the world using the Mercator Projection

Web Mercator Auxiliary Sphere is the projection that has become industry accepted on the Internet for web-based mapping. Simply put, it is a Mercator projection used across the Web, using WGS 84 as the reference datum.

Altitude, Course, and Speed

If you had to rank geolocation properties by importance, the latitude and longitude of a position would obviously be the most important. As I explained earlier, however, there is a third component that makes up every point in a geographic coordinate system: *altitude*, also known as *elevation* or *height*. Beyond this, there are additional components that, though not strictly necessary, can be very useful pieces of data for a geolocation application. These components are related to one another and are useful when the object being located is moving—*course* and *speed*.

Geodetic Height

Without an elevation, a point cannot be pinpointed exactly on a topographic feature. This height, when discussed in reference to a geolocation, is generally understood to be above sea level, though it does not have to be defined this way. As our technologies advance and more diverse environments open up to us, it is quite possible that we will find uses for geolocation below the ocean's surface as well as above it. In fact, there are two ways that elevation can be defined in a datum—either by sea level or by geodesy.

Vertical Datum

The usual method for measuring a height on land is based off the Mean Sea Level (MSL) of the Earth, seen in Figure 2-4. By measuring the height of the ocean's surface over a long period of time, an average sea level can be calculated to remove tides and other oceanic effects. Local gravitational differences on the Earth, however, will still have an effect on the mean sea level in relation to the vertical datum. Because of this, individual countries choose a mean sea level at a particular point which they designate as their standard and use this for reference when doing localized mapping. In Canada, the United States, and Mexico, the localized point is in Quebec, Canada.

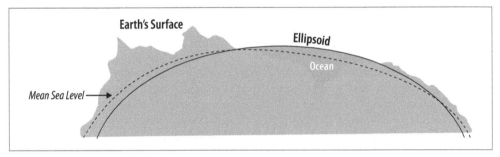

Figure 2-4. The Earth's height varies at any given point.

There are circumstances when using mean sea level does not provide the optimal reference for a vertical datum, and this comes into play when the topographical elements being plotted are of an historic nature. Sea levels do not remain constant with time, therefore a different vertical datum is usually referenced when dealing with this type of data. A geodetic datum arbitrarily assigns an elevation on the Earth's surface as "zero", without using the ocean as a guide. This point usually coincides with the localized point assigned by countries when defining mean sea level, but due to variations across the globe, the two "zeroes" will not coincide anywhere else. NAVD 88, used in North America, is an example of a geodetic vertical datum (and happens to have the same localized point in Quebec as the mean sea level point).

Course

An object's *course* is the proposed direction that it will take to get from one point to another. It can be defined as a planned route between two points, or it can be defined as the necessary path an object must take to get from one point to the next. A course is constructed out of straight lines between points, with each segment of the course being called a *leg*.

The *heading* of an object describes the direction that it is pointing in at any given time. The direction is measured as an angle, in degrees, relative to a fixed reference point which in most cases is True North. The angle is measured from 0° in a clockwise direction to 360°, where 0° is North, 90° is East, 180° is South, and 270° is West.

Course and heading are sometimes used interchangeably, though they do have slightly different meanings. The heading, as I just described, is the direction an object is *facing*, but not necessarily moving in. The course, meanwhile, is the *intended* direction of movement (think "plotting a course on a map" when traveling). Then there is the term *track*, which is another term you will hear when talking about heading and course. The track is the direction in a line between the point of origin (where you were when you started moving) and the present location. Another way to put it is that a track is a realized course.

Speed

Looking at everything we have discussed thus far in this chapter, speed may be the most obvious. As soon as I say *speed*, I am sure you are thinking. "how fast something is going?" That is exactly what I am talking about with respect to geolocation. Speed is simply the rate of motion of an object. I know this is an easy concept, so I do not want the physics that follows to distract from that—I hope it does not.

From a physics or mathematics perspective, a better definition for speed is the *magnitude* of an object's *velocity*, where the velocity of an object is a measurement of the rate of change in the position of the object in a given direction. Speed and velocity both consider the length the object travels and the time it takes to travel that distance, measured in *meters per second* (this is the standard unit declared by the International System of Units (SI)).

The average speed of an object (V) is defined as:

    V = d / t

where d is the total distance traveled and t is the total time taken.

This should not be confused with the *instantaneous speed*, or speed at any given time, of an object (v), which is calculated as the time derivative of s, where s is the length of the path traveled until time t:

    v = ds / dt

Though the SI unit of speed is meters per second, more familiar units of measure (ones used in cars every day) are units like miles per hours and kilometers per hour.

Accuracy

In a perfect world, the location you are given when requesting geolocation information would be exactly right—meaning where it says you are is where you actually are. Well, the world is not perfect (I apologize if I burst someone's bubble there). The reality of the situation is that the accuracy of the data will fluctuate each and every time a geolocation request is made. There are so many factors that go into giving a location that when you stop and think about the mechanisms behind geolocation, it is pretty amazing that we have the accuracy we do.

Before I go any further, let me define *accuracy*—the accuracy of a geolocation is how close a location measures to its actual location. A common way to use accuracy in GIS is to state that "a point is accurate within 20 meters," meaning that the actual location of the point is no more than 20 meters away from the location we are showing for that point. Figure 2-5 gives an example of a point with different radii of accuracy surrounding it.

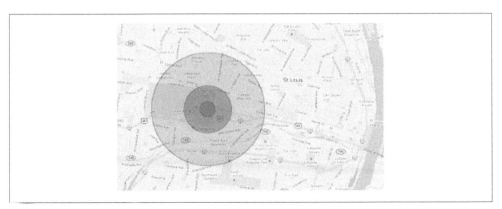

Figure 2-5. Example radii of accuracy for a given point.

One of the main factors for a geolocation's accuracy is the way in which the location was gathered. An IP address is less accurate than a Cell ID, which is less accurate than GPS. Why? The most obvious reason for the inaccuracy of an IP address is that the location could be gathered from the IP address of a router or firewall that is miles away from the computer browser that the geolocation was requested from. This type of situation would be fairly common in a large corporate environment. Cell IDs are generally more accurate than IP addresses as a triangulation must be calculated from cell towers in order to get a geolocation. GPS is generally more accurate than Cell IDs because there are more complex calculations going on to get a geolocation from more satellites.

Of course, hardware glitches, radio interference, weather, and so on can degrade signals and decrease the accuracy of any geolocation request at any time. That is why it is important to gather accuracy information whenever a geolocation request is made, so that the user can be made aware of potential errors in their location in an application. The accuracy of geolocation information will get better as technology continues to get more sophisticated, but even the most technologically sound implementations will be subject to things outside of the manufacturer's hands.

## CHAPTER 3

Geolocation API in Code

At this point, I am sure there are a lot of you reading this that are thinking to yourself, "Thank you, Mr. Author, for all of that lovely background information on what geolocation is, but can we see how to do this in code, already?" If that is you, then you are in luck, because this chapter is all about coding with the W3C Geolocation API.

The background information in the previous chapters is definitely relevant to our discussion on the Geolocation API itself. Understanding, for example, that the *latitude* and *longitude* that we retrieve from the user's browser is in the WGS 84 datum will come in handy. If you have no idea what I am talking about, go back and read (or re-read) Chapter 2 so that you have a good grasp on the information we are going to be working with.

W3C Geolocation API

The *W3C Geolocation API* is a specification that provides scripted access to geographical location information associated with the hosting device.[*] It is meant to be a "high-level interface" so that the developer using it does not need to worry about details such as how the location information is being gathered. It does not matter whether the device is using GPS, IP Address, or Cell ID; only the geolocation information itself is important. The one caveat that the specification makes, however, is that there is no guarantee that the location returned from the API is the actual location of the device. This should come as no surprise, given that GPS may not have enough visible satellites to determine an accurate position, there may not be enough cell towers to get a proper triangulation from a Cell ID, or an IP Address could be spoofed to give a completely false location. Because of these, and other possible reasons, the developer may feel reasonably confident in the results returned by the API, but should never rely on any information blindly.

---

[*] *Geolocation API Specification: W3C Candidate Recommendation 07 September 2010.* Editor, Andrei Popescu, Google, Inc. *http://www.w3.org/TR/geolocation-API/.*

The latest version of the W3C Geolocation API Specification is W3C Candidate Recommendation 07 September 2010.

Current API Support

Currently, the W3C Geolocation API is supported by most modern browsers on both the desktop and on mobile phones. Table 3-1 shows the current browser support for the API. The biggest issue developers will face is that older browsers have obviously not adopted this technology since it was created after those browsers were released. This is particularly difficult for developers because of the widespread use of Internet Explorer 8 (and perhaps even Internet Explorer 7), and also for all users of mobile phones who have not upgraded to current versions of software or hardware. The good news is that the API should be available in all future browser and phone releases.

Table 3-1. Browser Support for the W3C Geolocation API

Web browser	Supported in versions
Firefox	3.5+
Chrome	5.0+
Internet Explorer	9.0+
Safari	5.0+[a]
Opera	10.6+
iPhone	3.1+
Android	2.0+
BlackBerry	6+[a]

[a] Has correct implementation, but not completely implemented

Other Browser Solutions

As I noted, not all browsers support the W3C Geolocation API, and these legacy browsers never will natively. Fortunately, other programmers have taken it upon themselves to do something about it, and wrote wrapper libraries that give these browsers most of the functionality found in the Geolocation API. However, there are differences between these libraries and the W3C Geolocation API which make it a bit more challenging for the developer to write code that will work in all browsers. First, let us take a look at some of these other APIs, and then we will see how we can resolve our differences.

Gears

Gears (*http://gears.google.com/*), formally known as Google Gears, is (as the name ob-viously suggests) a code library written by the good folks over at Google, Inc. Gears is designed to be an open source project that enables more powerful web applications by adding new features to the web browser. The component of Gears that most interests us is the *Geolocation module*, which acts very much like the W3C Geolocation API. In fact, parts of the W3C's Geolocation API were probably modeled on Gears.

 In the Gears API Blog (*http://gearsblog.blogspot.com/2011/03/stopping -gears.html*) on March 11, 2011, Google announced that no further new releases to Gears would be coming, nor would Gears support newer browsers such as Firefox 4 and Internet Explorer 9, and it will be re-moved from Chrome 12. Older browsers, however, can continue to use Gears to gain the functionality they lack.

Gears can be added to a web page using the following line of code:

```
<script type="text/javascript"
    src="http://code.google.com/apis/gears/gears_init.js"></script>
```

We do not need to worry about the specifics of using Gears in our code because, as you will see in "geo-location-javascript" on page 34 we will let another library take care of reconciling differences between Gears, other APIs, and the W3C Geolocation API. Additional examples can be found in Chapter 4, but for now, just remember that this library is out there and available.

Other Mobile APIs

Of course, hardware vendors have their own specifications and APIs for using geolo-cation on their devices, especially for older mobile device platforms before geolocation became mainstream. The following lists some of the other Geolocation APIs that may be encountered or required depending on the devices connecting to your site:

- iOS
- BlackBerry
- Nokia
- webOS (Palm)

All iPhones with OS less than 3.0 relied on Apple's own Geolocation API for any location-based application development. The same holds true for BlackBerry developers—BlackBerry devices with OS less than 6 relied on BlackBerry's own implementation (*http://docs.blackberry.com/en/developers/deliverables/18446/Geolocation_Objects_12.*

Nokia has its own version of a Geolocation API (*http://www.forum.nokia.com/Develop/ Web/*) that works in the browser shipped with its phones, as does Palm with its webOS

2.1 SDK's HTML5 Enhancements (*http://developer.palm.com/index.php?option=com _content&view=article&id=2109#html5*). It is hoped that further development by these vendors will release fully W3C Geolocation API compliant browsers or support, which would eliminate the mess that developers currently face.

Which brings us to...

geo-location-javascript

geo-location-javascript (*http://code.google.com/p/geo-location-javascript/*) is an attempt to build a JavaScript framework that will wrap all of the underlying platform implementations into a single API that works similarly to the W3C Geolocation API Specification. The following platforms are currently supported by the API:

- iOS
- Android
- BlackBerry OS
- Gears
- Nokia Web Run-Time (WRT)
- webOS Application Platform (Palm)
- Torch Mobile Iris Browser
- Mozilla Geode

The API has two key functions: checking to see if the connecting device has geolocation capabilities and getting the location of the device. As you will see in "The W3C Geolocation API Does More" on page 35, this is just a small subset of functionality that the full W3C Geolocation API has, and there is additional coding work needed if you want that additional functionality.

Consider the following code snippet:

```
<script type="text/javascript"
    src="http://code.google.com/apis/gears/gears_init.js"></script>
<script type="text/javascript" src="geo.js"></script>
<script type="text/javascript">
  function initialize() {
    if (geo_position_js.init())
      geo_position_js.getCurrentPosition(show_position, error_handler,
        { enableHighAccuracy: true }
      );
    else
      alert('Geolocation functionality is not available.');
</script>
```

The first line of code loads Gears into the application, and the following line loads the geo-location-javascript API. In a real application scenario, the `initialize()` function would be called on an `onload` event fired by the document.

The `initialize()` function itself is straightforward. It first checks to see if the device supports geolocation, and if it does it acquires the current position of the device. Should the device not support geolocation, then a message to that effect will be displayed to the user. The geo-location-javascript API, like all other Geolocation APIs, including the W3C Geolocation API, requires the user to opt in and allow the location to be collected before proceeding. Learn more about that in "Privacy" on page 45.

There are two callback functions in the call to `geo_position_js.getCurrentPosi tion()`: `show_position` and `error_handler`. If anything were to go wrong with the attempt to locate the device, or the user opted out of the location search, the `error_han dler` function would be called. Otherwise, the `show_position` function would be called, and the *latitude* and *longitude* of the device would be available to the application.

 As previously mentioned, the geo-location-javascript API does not have support for a position polling method like the W3C Geolocation API does (discussed further in the next section). You will need to use a Java-Script `setInterval()` and poll the `getCurrentPosition()` yourself.

The W3C Geolocation API Does More

In this chapter, and the book in general, the focus is on a JavaScript implementation of the W3C Geolocation API to work within HTML5 applications. The interface's implementation is being included in all modern browsers for both desktop and mobile devices. Because it is a newer API, however, there has been a need for other APIs to step in and create the cross-browser implementations needed to include older devices and browsers. The geo-location-javascript API, described in "geo-location-java-script" on page 34, is one such API.

The downside to using these APIs is they do not share all the functionality that the W3C Geolocation API has, leaving gaps in what can be developed. As you will see in the rest of this chapter, the W3C Geolocation API is a robust and thorough interface that allows for the development of web applications that rival applications created natively on devices.

The Geolocation Object

The W3C Geolocation API specifies a general implementation for the objects, properties, and methods associated with the *Geolocation* interface. One object holds the whole implementation of the W3C Geolocation API—the *Geolocation* object. This object can be used within JavaScript to gather geolocation information about the device on which the browser resides. The *Geolocation* object is a new property of the global `window.nav igator` *Browser* Object, and can be accessed from the `window.navigator.geolocation` instantiation.

As with all JavaScript objects, it is a best practice to first test for the existence of an object's implementation within a browser before using it, as the following code illustrates:

```
if (window.navigator.geolocation) {
    // do some geolocation stuff
} else {
    // the browser does not natively support geolocation
}
```

In the preceding code, the existence of an implementation of the geolocation property is tested, and if it exists, the code will do geolocation processing, otherwise something else will need to be tried.

The *Geolocation* object contains three public methods, as described in Table 3-2. All geolocation functionality stems from these methods and the callback functions they take as parameters.

Table 3-2. Geolocation methods

Method	Description
clearWatch(watchId)	Stops the watch process associated with the passed *watchId*.
getCurrentPosition(successCallback, [errorCallback, [options]])	Attempt to gather geolocation information, calling *successCallback* when it succeeds or the optional *errorCallback* when it fails.
watchPosition(successCallback, [errorCallback, [options]])	Attempts to gather geolocation information at regular intervals, calling *successCallback* when it succeeds or the optional *errorCallback* when it fails.

Get the User's Position

Once it has been verified that the browser supports the W3C Geolocation API, requests can be made to get the current position of the device in question. This is done using the getCurrentPosition() method. The getCurrentPosition() method requires at least one parameter, a position callback function. Optionally, it can also take an error callback function, and an options parameter. It is called like this:

```
navigator.geolocation.getCurrentPosition(successCallback, errorCallback,
    options);
```

The first parameter, successCallback, will be called when a successful position has been discovered by the inner workings of the API. The second parameter, errorCallback, is optional and will be called when there is an error in gathering a position. The final parameter, options, is a *PositionOptions* object that is also optional.

 The successCallback parameter for the getCurrentPosition() callback is required—if it is omitted, the getCurrentPosition() call automatically fails and aborts any location fetching.

The following code snippet shows the getCurrentPosition() more fully:

```
if (window.navigator.geolocation) {
  navigator.geolocation.getCurrentPosition(successCallback, errorCallback,
      options);
} else {
  alert('Your browser does not natively support geolocation.');
}

function successCallback(position) {
  // Do something with a location here
}

function errorCallback(error) {
  // There was a problem getting the location
}
```

PositionOptions

The *PositionOptions* object is an optional parameter that can be passed to the getCurrentPosition() method, and as you will see in "Update the User's Position" on page 38, is also an optional parameter to the watchPosition() method. All of the properties available in the *PositionOptions* object, shown in Table 3-3, are optional as well.

Table 3-3. PositionOptions object properties

Property	JavaScript type	Description
enableHighAccuracy	Boolean	Flags the API to attempt to get as close to the exact location of the device as possible. The default value is false. Slower response times and/or increased power consumption may result from setting this property to true.
maximumAge	Integer	Signals to the application that it will accept a cached position with an age no greater than the time specified in *milliseconds*. The default value is 0.
timeout	Integer	Indicates the maximum length of time, in *milliseconds*, that the application will wait from the beginning of a call to the evocation of the *successCallback* function. The default value is 0.

The following is an example of calling getCurrentPosition() with the *PositionOptions* object set:

```
var options = {
  enableHighAccuracy: true,
  maximumAge: 60000,
  timeout: 45000
};
```

```
navigator.geolocation.getCurrentPosition(successCallback, errorCallback,
    options);
```

This code calls getCurrentPosition(), requesting high accuracy, and a cached position no older than 60 seconds, with a timeout period of 45 seconds before returning an error.

Cached Positions

A *cached* position is a position that was gathered by the application sometime in the past that may be used again instead of requiring a new position to be fetched. When it is not necessary for the application to display changes in a position very frequently, a cached position is a good alternative. This will save processing overhead since a new call to the API will not be needed in order to get a cached position. To specify the acceptable age of a position, the *PositionOptions* object is passed to the getCurrentPosition() or watchPosition() method with the optional maximumAge property set to the desired time in milliseconds.

For example:

```
var options = {
  maximumAge: 600000
};

navigator.geolocation.getCurrentPosition(successCallback, errorCallback,
    options);
```

The preceding code would accept a cached position that no older than 60 minutes. If you wish to get a fresh position each time, do not pass a maximumAge property (it defaults to 0), or pass the value 0 yourself. Should you wish to always get a cached position, regardless of its age, pass the value Infinity to the calling method, like this:

```
var options = {
  maximumAge: Infinity
};

navigator.geolocation.getCurrentPosition(successCallback, errorCallback,
    options);
```

Update the User's Position

There are times when an application requires an updated position every time the device changes location. In these cases, a call to the watchPosition() method is warranted in place of calling the getCurrentPosition() method. The watchPosition() method has the same basic structure as the getCurrentPosition() method. It also takes a successCallback parameter that is required, as well as two optional parameters: errorCallback and options.

The major difference between the two methods is that the watchPosition() method will return a value immediately upon being called which uniquely identifies that *watch operation*. The watch operation itself is an *asynchronous* operation. It is called like this:

```
var watcher = navigator.geolocation.watchPosition(successCallback,
            errorCallback, options);
```

The first parameter, successCallback, will be called when a successful position has been gathered by the API. The second parameter, errorCallback, is optional and will be called when there is an error in gathering a position. The final parameter, options, is a *PositionOptions* object that is also optional. The variable, watcher, is the unique identifier for this particular watch operation.

The following code snippet shows how to use watchPosition():

```
var watcher = null;
var options = {
  enableHighAccuracy: true,
  timeout: 45000
};

if (window.navigator.geolocation) {
  watcher = navigator.geolocation.watchPosition(successCallback,
            errorCallback, options);
} else {
  alert('Your browser does not natively support geolocation.');
}

function successCallback(position) {
  // Do something with a location here
}

function errorCallback(error) {
  // There was a problem getting the location
}
```

No Need for Polling

The watchPosition() method has built-in functionality to automatically poll the device for a change in position and will call the successCallback function every time there is a new position for the device. This eliminates the need for the developer to roll her own code to poll the device every *x* number of seconds. Because the watchPosition() method has automatic polling, this also provides for true real-time geolocation applications. Creating custom polling functionality will give you pseudo-real-time position updates at best, and will cause additional processing overhead that will slow the application down in the long run.

Whenever possible, the watchPosition() method's polling capabilities should be used for position updating. Do not create custom position polling functionality unless your application has a unique need for it.

Clearing a Watch Operation

Like the JavaScript `clearTimeout()` and `clearInterval()` methods, the W3C Geolocation API provides a method for clearing a watch operation by passing the desired `watchId` to the `clearWatch()` method. The syntax is:

```
navigator.geolocation.clearWatch(watcher);
```

The following code demonstrates creating a new watch operation, and then removing that watch upon the successful fetching of a position:

```
var watcher = null;
var options = {
  enableHighAccuracy: true,
  timeout: 45000
};

if (window.navigator.geolocation) {
  watcher = navigator.geolocation.watchPosition(successCallback,
            errorCallback, options);
} else {
  alert('Your browser does not natively support geolocation.');
}

function successCallback(position) {
  navigator.geolocation.clearWatch(watcher);
  // Do something with a location here
}
```

Handling a Successful Request

Once a location request has been gathered by the API, the `successCallback` function is called. This works the same using either the `getCurrentPosition()` or `updatePosition()` methods. The `successCallback` function is passed one parameter from the API, a *Position* object.

Position Object

The *Position* object holds all of the geolocation information that is returned from the W3C Geolocation API call and is passed to a `successCallback` function. Table 3-4 contains a list of the current properties this object has. There is room in this object for additional information, and, in particular, geocoding information in possible future versions of the API.

Table 3-4. Position object properties

Property	Description
coords	A *Coordinates* object containing geographic coordinates and other properties.
timestamp	A *DOMTimeStamp* holding the time when the *Position* object was obtained.

Coordinates Object

The main geographic information gathered by the API is held in a *Coordinates* object which is a property of the *Position* object (see "Position Object" on page 40). This information is in the World Geodetic System reference system WGS 84. More information on this reference system can be found in "WGS 84" on page 25. Currently, no other reference system is supported by the W3C Geolocation API. A list of the properties found in the *Coordinates* object are in Table 3-5.

Table 3-5. Coordinates object properties

Property	Description
latitude	The geographic coordinate of latitude for the device, measured in decimal degrees.
longitude	The geographic coordinate of longitude for the device, measured in decimal degrees.
altitude	The geographic height of the device, measured in meters above the WGS 84 ellipsoid.
accuracy	The accuracy of the latitude and longitude, specified in meters.
altitudeAccuracy	The accruacy of the height, specified in meters. When not supported, this value is null.
heading	The direction of travel of the device, measured in degrees from 0° clockwise to 360°. This value will be NaN when the device is not moving. When not supported, this value is null.
speed	The current ground speed of the device, measured in meters per second. When not supported, this value is null.

In Example 3-1, all of the components of the *Geolocation* object covered so far are shown in use.

Example 3-1. A first geolocation example

```
<!DOCTYPE html>
<html lang="en">
  <head>
    <title>A First Geolocation Example</title>
    <meta name="viewport" content="initial-scale=1.0, user-scalable=no"/>
    <meta charset="utf-8"/>'
    <script type="text/javascript">
      var options = {
        enableHighAccuracy: true,
        maximumAge: 1000,
        timeout: 45000
      };

      if (window.navigator.geolocation) {
        navigator.geolocation.getCurrentPosition(successCallback,
            errorCallback, options);
      } else {
        alert('Your browser does not natively support geolocation.');
      }
```

```
    function successCallback(position) {
      var output = '';

      output += "Your position has been located.\n\n";
      output += 'Latitude: ' + position.coords.latitude + "°\n";
      output += 'Longitude: ' + position.coords.longitude + "°\n";
      output += 'Accuracy: ' + position.coords.accuracy + " meters\n";
      if (position.coords.altitude)
        output += 'Altitude: ' + position.coords.altitude + " meters\n";
      if (position.coords.altitudeAccuracy)
        output += 'Altitude Accuracy: ' + position.coords.altitudeAccuracy +
            " meters\n";
      if (position.coords.heading)
        output += 'Heading: ' + position.coords.Heading + "°\n";
      if (position.coords.speed)
        output += 'Speed: ' + position.coords.Speed + " m/s\n";
      output += 'Time of Position: ' + position.timestamp;

      alert(output);'
    }

    function errorCallback(error) {
      // There was a problem getting the location
    }
  </script>
</head>
<body>
  <div>A First Geolocation Example</div>
</body>
</html>
```

This example shows how to get all of the geographic information from the *Position* object, though it does not do anything more than alert the results to the user. In a real application, the coordinates would be used to plot a point on a map, or they could be saved to a database.

Converting Coordinates Programmatically

The latitude and longitude coordinates returned by the W3C Geolocation API are in a decimal degree format. There are times when it is helpful to have these degrees converted to a degree, minute, second format, without having to do so by hand each time. Example 3-2 provides two objects for doing conversions from decimal degrees to degrees, minutes, seconds (the *dd2dms* object) and vise versa (the *dms2dd* object).

Example 3-2. Converting from decimal degrees to DMS and back

```
function dd2dms(degree, lat_long) {
  this.deg = Math.abs(parseInt(degree));
  this.min = (Math.abs(degree) - this.deg) * 60;
  this.sec = this.min;
  this.min = Math.abs(parseInt(this.min));
  this.sec = Math.round((this.sec - this.min) * 60 * 1000000) / 1000000;
  this.sign = (degree < 0) ? -1 : 1;
  this.dir = (lat_long == 'lat') ? ((this.sign > 0) ? 'N' : 'S') :
```

```
        ((this.sign > 0) ? 'E' : 'W');
  this.toString = function(dir) {
    if (isNaN(dir))
      return (this.deg * this.sign) + "\u00b0 " + this.min + "' " +
          this.sec + '" ';
    else
      return this.deg + "\u00b0 " + this.min + "' " + this.sec + '" ' +
          this.dir;
  };
}

function dms2dd(deg, min, sec, dir) {
  if (dir) {
    this.sign = (dir.toLowerCase() == 'w' || dir.toLowerCase() == 's') ? -1 :
        1;
    this.dir = (dir.toLowerCase() == 'w' || dir.toLowerCase() == 's' ||
        dir.toLowerCase() == 'n' || dir.toLowerCase() == 'e') ?
        dir.toUpperCase() : '';
  } else {
    this.sign = (deg < 0) ? -1 : 1;
    this.dir = '';
  }
  this.dec = Math.round((Math.abs(deg) + ((min * 60) + sec) / 3600) *
      1000000) / 1000000;
  this.toString = function(dir) {
    if (isNaN(dir) || this.dir == '')
      return (this.dec * this.sign) + "\u00b0";
    else
      return this.dec + "\u00b0" + ' ' + this.dir;
  }
}
```

These are two simple objects that can be enhanced and tweaked for better performance, but they should give you an idea how to do these conversions in your own code. The following are examples of how you can use the objects to do conversions:

```
alert(new dd2dms(40.567534, 'long').toString(1)); // output: 40° 34' 3.1224" E
alert(new dms2dd(40, 34, 3.1224, 'E').toString(1)); // output: 40.567534° E
```

Handling an Error from the Request

There are several reasons why a location request could fail within the API, and with any of these the errorCallback function is called when it is provided with either the getCurrentPosition() or updatePosition() methods. When provided, the errorCall back function is passed one parameter from the API, a *PositionError* object.

PositionError Object

The *PositionError* object holds all of the error information returned from the W3C Geolocation API call and is passed to an errorCallback function. Table 3-6 contains a list of this object's current properties.

Table 3-6. PositionError object properties

Property	Description
code	The *code* is a numeric value alerting the developer to what the error is. The code will be one of the following values:
	PERMISSION_DENIED (1)
	The location call failed because the application does not have the necessary permissions to use the Geolocation API.
	POSITION_UNAVAILALE (2)
	The location call failed because the device could not determine a position.
	TIMEOUT (2)
	The location call failed because the length of time elapsed making attempting to find a position exceeded the value of the timeout property.
message	A detailed *message* containing the error that was encountered for the purposes of developer debugging. This message is not meant to be displayed to the end-user of the application.

In Example 3-3, a final version of the *Geolocation* object using all of the API is shown.

Example 3-3. A second geolocation example

```
<!DOCTYPE html>
<html lang="en">
  <head>
    <title>A First Geolocation Example</title>
    <meta name="viewport" content="initial-scale=1.0, user-scalable=no"/>
    <meta charset="utf-8"/>
    <script type="text/javascript">
      var options = {
        enableHighAccuracy: true,
        maximumAge: 1000,
        timeout: 45000
      };

      if (window.navigator.geolocation) {
        navigator.geolocation.getCurrentPosition(successCallback,
            errorCallback, options);
      } else {
        alert('Your browser does not natively support geolocation.');
      }

      function successCallback(position) {
        var output = '';

        output += "Your position has been located.\n\n";
        output += 'Latitude: ' + position.coords.latitude + "°\n";
        output += 'Longitude: ' + position.coords.longitude + "°\n";
        output += 'Accuracy: ' + position.coords.accuracy + " meters\n";
        if (position.coords.altitude)
          output += 'Altitude: ' + position.coords.altitude + " meters\n";
        if (position.coords.altitudeAccuracy)
```

```
        output += 'Altitude Accuracy: ' + position.coords.altitudeAccuracy +
            " meters\n";
    if (position.coords.heading)
        output += 'Heading: ' + position.coords.Heading + "°\n";
    if (position.coords.speed)
        output += 'Speed: ' + position.coords.Speed + " m/s\n";
    output += 'Time of Position: ' + position.timestamp;

    alert(output);
    }

    function errorCallback(error) {
      switch (error.code) {
        case error.PERMISSION_DENIED:
          alert('You have denied access to your position.');
          break;
        case error.POSITION_UNAVAILABLE:
          alert('There was a problem getting your position.');
          break;
        case error.TIMEOUT:
          alert('The application has timed out attempting to get your ' +
              location.');
            break;
      }
    }
  </script>
  </head>
  <body>
    <div>A First Geolocation Example</div>
  </body>
</html>
```

In this example, the errors are captured, and a more user-friendly **alert** is sent to the user. In a real application, it would be good to log the error, and possibly do more with the message for the user, but this should give you some idea of what to do with the error code being passed with the *PositionError* object.

Privacy

Privacy is an important matter, not only with the W3C Geolocation API, but with all geolocation applications available today. Companies know how dearly individuals hold their privacy, and take many precautions to safeguard any data collected from the user. If a user is ever in any doubt as to a company's policies and procedures, he should check with the company's *Privacy Policy* regarding user data.

To address security and privacy considerations with the W3C Geolocation API, the specification outlines that no locations may be sent to web applications without the express permission of the user. The standard way this is being implemented across browsers is to provide an information bar that, as per the W3C specification, lists the URI of the document requesting a location (see Figure 3-1). The user can opt to always

Figure 3-1. Opt-in policy in Chrome

allow access for the site with a checkbox indicating this site-level access, which can be undone at any time within the settings of the browser itself.

From a development standpoint, should the user decide not to grant your application access to his location information, you should make sure that your application can handle this gracefully.

Unless the user has granted the application a site-level access retained within the specific browser, the permissions given by the user will expire at the end of the current browsing session. With such opt-in policies, any implementation of the W3C Geolocation API should achieve adequate privacy functionality and alleviate a user's anxiety towards their location data. The best a developer can do is guarantee proper handling of a user's data, while users would be wise to follow a policy of only granting access to their personal data to trusted individuals and sites.

## CHAPTER 4

Geolocation and Mapping APIs

Chapter 3 introduced us to using the W3C Geolocation API to collect location information from the user's browser with JavaScript code. Although that is the whole point of this book, it is not extremely useful to collect geolocation information unless you, the developer, are going to do something with it. One effective application for collecting a user's location is to place that point on a map. Let's face it, mapping a location (or multiple locations) is a common thing to do in the world of GIS.

There are many solutions available for web-mapping applications—Google Maps JavaScript API V3 (*http://code.google.com/apis/maps/documentation/javascript/*), Bing Maps AJAX Control, Version 7.0 (*http://msdn.microsoft.com/en-us/library/gg427610.aspx*), Esri ArcGIS JavaScript API 2.2 (*http://help.arcgis.com/en/webapi/javascript/arcgis/*), Yahoo Maps AJAX API (*http://developer.yahoo.com/maps/ajax/*), and OpenStreetMap API v0.6 (*http://wiki.openstreetmap.org/wiki/API_v0.6*) to name a few (more than a few actually). Most of the APIs available to do web mapping are very similar in nature. Because of this, I have decided to focus on just a couple of the APIs available, and leave it up to you to pick the API that best suits your needs.

After giving you a taste of these APIs for use in your applications, we can then explore what to do with the information you have collected so that it can be referenced by other applications or replotted in the future. This is as important as being able to map the geolocations being collected, since most GIS applications are going to be interested in more than a single user's point information. To this end, we will look at different ways to save our geolocation information so that it can be consumed by these other applications.

A Google Maps Example

The Google Maps JavaScript API lets you embed Google Maps in your own web pages. Version 3 of this API is especially designed to be faster and more applicable to mobile devices, as well as traditional desktop browser applications.* With this API, it is easy for a developer to embed a map that functions just like the *http://maps.google.com/* web page, and to customize its look and functionality to suit the needs of the application being built. It is a very popular API for building web applications, currently being used in over 150,000 websites.[†]

The Google Maps API, Briefly

For the purposes of this book, I have included all of the code for the Google Maps application into a single HTML file to make it easier to read. If I were to create an actual application, I would break the Cascading Style Sheet (CSS) rules and JavaScript into their own files (perhaps multiple files should the application be more complex) as a better programming practice.

Take a look at the code in Example 4-1, which contains everything needed to create a simple Google Map application.

Example 4-1. A simple Google Map

```
<!DOCTYPE html>
<html lang="en">
  <head>
    <title>A Simple Google Map</title>
    <meta name="viewport" content="initial-scale=1.0, user-scalable=no"/>
    <meta charset="utf-8"/>
    <style type="text/css">
      html { height: 100% }
      body { height: 100%; margin: 0; padding: 0 }
      #map { height: 100% }
    </style>
    <script type="text/javascript"
        src="http://maps.google.com/maps/api/js?sensor=false"></script>
    <script type="text/javascript">
      var map;

      /* This is called once the page has loaded */
      function InitMap() {
        /* Set all of the options for the map */
        var options = {
          zoom: 4,
          center: new google.maps.LatLng(38.6201, -90.2003),
          mapTypeId: google.maps.MapTypeId.ROADMAP,
          mapTypeControl: true,
          mapTypeControlOptions: {
            style: google.maps.MapTypeControlStyle.HORIZONTAL_BAR,
            position: google.maps.ControlPosition.BOTTOM_CENTER
          },
          panControl: true,
          panControlOptions: {
            position: google.maps.ControlPosition.TOP_RIGHT
```

---

[*] *Google Maps JavaScript API V3. http://code.google.com/apis/maps/documentation/javascript/.*

[†] *Mapping Success: Google Maps Case Studies. http://maps.google.com/help/maps/casestudies/.*

```
          },
          zoomControl: true,
          zoomControlOptions: {
            style: google.maps.ZoomControlStyle.LARGE,
            position: google.maps.ControlPosition.LEFT_CENTER
          },
          scaleControl: true,
          scaleControlOptions: {
            position: google.maps.ControlPosition.BOTTOM_LEFT
          },
          streetViewControl: true,
          streetViewControlOptions: {
            position: google.maps.ControlPosition.LEFT_TOP
          }
        };

        /* Create a new Map for the application */
        map = new google.maps.Map(document.getElementById('map'), options);
      }

      /* A utility object for simple event handlilng */
      var Utils = { };

      Utils.addEvent = (function() {
        return function addEvent(eventObj, event, eventHandler) {
          if (eventObj.addEventListener) {
            eventObj.addEventListener(event, eventHandler, false);
          } else if (eventObj.attachEvent) {
            event = 'on' + event;
            eventObj.attachEvent(event, eventHandler);
          } else {
            eventObj['on' + event] = function() { eventHandler() };
          }
        };
      }());

      Utils.removeEvent = (function() {
        return function removeEvent(event) {
          if (event.preventDefault) {
            event.preventDefault();
            event.stopProgagation();
          } else {
            event.returnValue = false;
            event.cancelBubble = true;
          }
        };
      }());

      Utils.addEvent(window, 'load', InitMap);
    </script>
  </head>
  <body>
    <div id="map"></div>
  </body>
</html>
```

The code in Example 4-1 produces a map like that shown in Figure 4-1. I will step through this code in more detail in a moment, but there are several things that should be noted right away:

- The application is written in HTML5.

- The Google Maps JavaScript API is included in the application by calling it from Google's site.

- There are a couple of utility JavaScript functions that aid in cross-browser compliant event handling.

- A Google Map is created by specifying the container, a `<div>` element, to hold the map, and a set of options that allow the developer to customize the look of the map's controls.

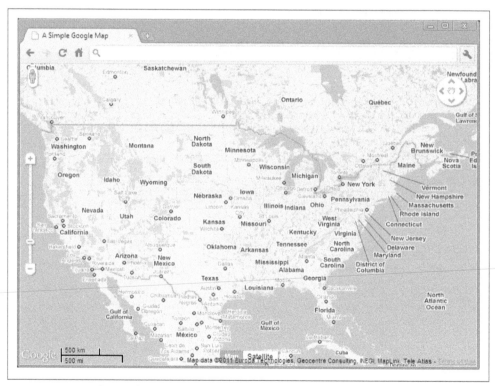

Figure 4-1. A simple Google Map in Chrome

Specifying a DOCTYPE in the application guarantees that browsers will render in standards-compliant mode, making it more cross-browser friendly. I chose HTML5 as it will soon be the industry standard, but any true DOCTYPE may be used.

The Google Maps JavaScript API is included in the application with the following line:

```
<script type="text/javascript"
    src="http://maps.google.com/maps/api/js?sensor=false"></script>
```

This makes the latest version of the API available for the application. The parameter `sensor` is set to *false* to indicate that the map is not using a sensor to determine the user's location.

 When geolocation is added to Example 4-1, the value of the `sensor` parameter will be changed to *true* so that the API knows that a location will be gathered by a "sensor," like the GPS locator in a phone.

Lastly, before looking at the Google Map JavaScript API specific code, the `<meta>` element specifying a `viewport` is recognized only by the iPhone right now, and tells it to set the application to full-screen and not allow the user to resize the application. Other smartphones may take advantage of this element in the future.

The `Utils` variable is nothing more than an object that holds cross-browser event handling functions that are used to create a more flexible application. By using the `Utils.addEvent()` method, this code can be plugged into an existing application and the developer does not have to worry about overwriting an existing `onload` function that may already be present. If a JavaScript library like jQuery or Dojo is being used in the application, then it will most likely have built-in methods that also take the hassle out of cross-browser event handling.

A *Map* is created by instantiating a new `google.maps.Map` object and specifying the element that will contain the map. The element is referenced using the `document.getElementById()` DOM method. The *Map* object also takes an *options* object that controls everything else about the map.

Map Options

By default, the Google Maps JavaScript API provides controls that enable basic map navigation and type switching. In addition, all devices have keyboard handling on by default. The default controls can be disabled using the *Map*'s `disableDefaultUI` property, and individual controls can be manipulated using their corresponding properties.

In Example 4-1, the following controls were configured for the map:

zoom
> The default zoom level was set to *4* in the example. The zoom property can range from *0* to *21+*, where *0* is a view of the whole world, and *21* is down to individual buildings.

center
> Defines the center of the map by a pair of coordinates.

mapType
> The Google Maps JavaScript API makes the following map types available: ROAD MAP, SATELLITE, HYBRID, and TERRAIN.

mapTypeControl, panControl, zoomControl, scaleControl, streetViewControl
> These controls are toggled on or off with values of *true* and *false*. In addition, each has specific configuration options along with a position property.

For more information on options available for the *Map* object, visit the Google Maps JavaScript API V3 Developer's Guide (*http://code.google.com/apis/maps/documenta tion/javascript/basics.html*) and API Reference (*http://code.google.com/apis/maps/docu mentation/javascript/reference.html*) .

Adding Geolocation to Google Maps

As we saw in Chapter 3, there are three main components needed in order to add geolocation to the Google map in Example 4-1: a call to getCurrentPosition(), a *successCallback* function to do something with the position when we get it, and an *errorCallback* function in case something goes wrong. We will create a function called getLocation() to handle checking for the navigator.geolocation object and for making our initial call for a location. This function will take advantage of a global variable called browserSupport that will eventually let our *errorCallback* function know if the error is from the API or a lack of browser support. I am doing this so that all of our error handling is in one function instead of having error alerts spread throughout the code. This way, if I choose to do something more robust with my error handling other than simply alert the user to a problem, all of the error code is in one place.

Example 4-2 illustrates this new functionality implemented into our Google Map example. Note that changes and additions to the code are highlighted in bold for easier identification.

Example 4-2. Adding geolocation to a Google Map

```
<!DOCTYPE html>
<html lang="en">
  <head>
    <title>Adding Geolocation to a Google Map</title>
    <meta name="viewport" content="initial-scale=1.0, user-scalable=no"/>
    <meta charset="utf-8"/>
    <style type="text/css">
      html { height: 100% } -
      body { height: 100%; margin: 0; padding: 0 }
      #map { height: 100% }
    </style>
    <script type="text/javascript"
        src="http://maps.google.com/maps/api/js?sensor=true"></script>
    <script type="text/javascript">
      var map;
      var browserSupport = false;
      var attempts = 0;
```

```javascript
/* This is called once the page has loaded */
function InitMap() {
  /* Set all of the options for the map */
  var options = {
    zoom: 4,
    center: new google.maps.LatLng(38.6201, -90.2003),
    mapTypeId: google.maps.MapTypeId.ROADMAP,
    mapTypeControl: true,
    mapTypeControlOptions: {
      style: google.maps.MapTypeControlStyle.HORIZONTAL_BAR,
      position: google.maps.ControlPosition.BOTTOM_CENTER
    },
    panControl: true,
    panControlOptions: {
      position: google.maps.ControlPosition.TOP_RIGHT
    },
    zoomControl: true,
    zoomControlOptions: {
      style: google.maps.ZoomControlStyle.LARGE,
      position: google.maps.ControlPosition.LEFT_CENTER
    },
    scaleControl: true,
    scaleControlOptions: {
      position: google.maps.ControlPosition.BOTTOM_LEFT
    },
    streetViewControl: true,
    streetViewControlOptions: {
      position: google.maps.ControlPosition.LEFT_TOP
    }
  };

  /* Create a new Map for the application */
  map = new google.maps.Map(document.getElementById('map'), options);

  /* Add Geolocation */
  getLocation();
}

/*
 * If the W3C Geolocation object is available then get the current
 * location, otherwise report the problem
 */
function getLocation() {
  /* Check if the browser supports the W3C Geolocation API */
  if (navigator.geolocation) {
    browserSupport = true;
    navigator.geolocation.getCurrentPosition(plotLocation,
        reportProblem, { timeout: 45000 });
  } else
    reportProblem();
}

/* Plot the location on the map and zoom to it */
function plotLocation(position) {
```

```
    attempts = 0;

    var point = new google.maps.LatLng(position.coords.latitude,
        position.coords.longitude);
    var marker = new google.maps.Marker({
      position: point
    });

    marker.setMap(map);
    map.setCenter(point);
    map.setZoom(15);
}

/* Report any errors using this function */
function reportProblem(e) {
  /* Is this a support issue or an API issue? */
  if (browserSupport) {
    switch (e.code) {
      case e.PERMISSION_DENIED:
        alert('You have denied access to your position. You will ' +
            'not get the most out of the application now.');
        break;
      case e.POSITION_UNAVAILABLE:
        alert('There was a problem getting your position.');
        break;
      case e.TIMEOUT:
        /* Three changes to get the location before a true timeout */
        if (++attempts < 3) {
          navigator.geolocation.getCurrentPosition(plotLocation,
              reportProblem);
        } else
          alert('The application has timed out attempting to get ' +
              'your location.');
          break;
      default:
        alert('There was a horrible Geolocation error that has ' +
            'not been defined.');
    }
  } else
    alert('Geolocation is not supported by your browser.');
}

/* A utility object for simple event handlilng */
var Utils = { };

Utils.addEvent = (function() {
  return function addEvent(eventObj, event, eventHandler) {
    if (eventObj.addEventListener) {
      eventObj.addEventListener(event, eventHandler, false);
    } else if (eventObj.attachEvent) {
      event = 'on' + event;
      eventObj.attachEvent(event, eventHandler);
    } else {
      eventObj['on' + event] = function() { eventHandler() };
    }
```

```
      };
    }());

    Utils.removeEvent = (function() {
      return function removeEvent(event) {
        if (event.preventDefault) {
          event.preventDefault();
          event.stopProgagation();
        } else {
          event.returnValue = false;
          event.cancelBubble = true;
        }
      };
    }());

    Utils.addEvent(window, 'load', InitMap);
  </script>
 </head>
 <body>
  <div id="map"></div>
 </body>
</html>
```

The first thing to note in this example is that sensor=true when we make the call to the Google JavaScript API, since we are using geolocation in this example. The getLocation() function is called right after our map object is instantiated.

Next, we define our two callback functions: plotLocation() and reportProblem(). plotLocation() will be passed a *Position* object that will contain all of the geolocation information, while reportProblem() will be passed a *PositionError* object that will contain an error code and message.

The plotLocation() function creates a *LatLng* object based on the passed latitude and longitude of the *Position* object, and from that *LatLng* object a *Marker* object is created. The *Marker* is placed on the map, and then the map is centered and zoomed to the current geolocation.

The reportProblem() function, meanwhile, simply alerts the user to the specific error the application has, based either on the browserSupport variable, or the *PositionError* code that is passed to the function. If the error is a timeout, the application will make three attempts at getting the current position of the user before giving up and reporting a problem.

Adding Geolocation for Other Browsers

The code in Example 4-2 works for browsers that support the W3C Geolocation API, but what about browsers that do not? Remember back in Chapter 1 when I discussed other browser solutions, and in particular "geo-location-javascript" on page 34? There are severe limitations to the geolocation functionality that this JavaScript library gives, but it is one solution that attempts cross-browser compatibility. Our Google Maps example is simple enough that we can use this library and not worry too much about the lack of functionality. Example 4-3 shows implementing a cross-browser geolocation solution using the geo-location-javascript library. Again, changes and additions to the code are highlighted in bold for easier identification.

Example 4-3. Adding geolocation for other browsers to a Google Map

```html
<!DOCTYPE html>
<html lang="en">
  <head>
    <title>Adding Geolocation for Other Browsers to a Google Map</title>
    <meta name="viewport" content="initial-scale=1.0, user-scalable=no"/>
    <meta charset="utf-8"/>
    <style type="text/css">
      html { height: 100% }
      body { height: 100%; margin: 0; padding: 0 }
      #map { height: 100% }
    </style>
    <script type="text/javascript"
        src="http://maps.google.com/maps/api/js?sensor=true"></script>
    <script type="text/javascript" src="gears_init.js"></script>
    <script type="text/javascript" src="geo.js"></script>
    <script type="text/javascript">
      var map;
      var browserSupport = false;

      /* This is called once the page has loaded */
      function InitMap() {
        /* Set all of the options for the map */
        var options = {
          zoom: 4,
          center: new google.maps.LatLng(38.6201, -90.2003),
          mapTypeId: google.maps.MapTypeId.ROADMAP,
          mapTypeControl: true,
          mapTypeControlOptions: {
            style: google.maps.MapTypeControlStyle.HORIZONTAL_BAR,
            position: google.maps.ControlPosition.BOTTOM_CENTER
          },
          panControl: true,
          panControlOptions: {
            position: google.maps.ControlPosition.TOP_RIGHT
          },
          zoomControl: true,
          zoomControlOptions: {
            style: google.maps.ZoomControlStyle.LARGE,
            position: google.maps.ControlPosition.LEFT_CENTER
          },
          scaleControl: true,
          scaleControlOptions: {
            position: google.maps.ControlPosition.BOTTOM_LEFT
          },
          streetViewControl: true,
          streetViewControlOptions: {
            position: google.maps.ControlPosition.LEFT_TOP
          }
        };
```

```
  /* Create a new Map for the application */
  map = new google.maps.Map(document.getElementById('map'), options);

  /* Add Geolocation */
  getLocation();
}

/*
 * The browser will now use whatever geolocation API is available to
 * it; hopefully it will be the W3C Geolocation object that is used to
 * get the current location. If there is no geolocation support at all,
 * then report the problem.
 */
function getLocation() {
  /* Check if the browser supports any geolocation API */
  if (geo_position_js.init()) {
    browserSupport = true;
    geo_position_js.getCurrentPosition(plotLocation,
        reportProblem);
  } else
    reportProblem();
}

/* Plot the location on the map and zoom to it */
function plotLocation(position) {
  var point = new google.maps.LatLng(position.coords.latitude,
      position.coords.longitude);
  var marker = new google.maps.Marker({
    position: point
  });

  marker.setMap(map);
  map.setCenter(point);
  map.setZoom(15);
}

/* Report any errors using this function */
function reportProblem() {
  /* Is this a support issue or an API issue? */
  if (browserSupport)
    alert('Could not locate your device.');
  else
    alert('Geolocation is not supported by your browser.');
}

/* A utility object for simple event handlilng */
var Utils = { };

Utils.addEvent = (function() {
  return function addEvent(eventObj, event, eventHandler) {
    if (eventObj.addEventListener) {
      eventObj.addEventListener(event, eventHandler, false);
    } else if (eventObj.attachEvent) {
      event = 'on' + event;
```

```
        eventObj.attachEvent(event, eventHandler);
      } else {
        eventObj['on' + event] = function() { eventHandler() };
      }
    };
  }());

  Utils.removeEvent = (function() {
    return function removeEvent(event) {
      if (event.preventDefault) {
        event.preventDefault();
        event.stopProgagation();
      } else {
        event.returnValue = false;
        event.cancelBubble = true;
      }
    };
  }());

  Utils.addEvent(window, 'load', InitMap);
    </script>
  </head>
  <body>
    <div id="map"></div>
  </body>
</html>
```

Calls to `gears_init.js` and `geo.js` load the libraries we are using for geolocation in this example. All of the *Map* functionality remains the same as in Example 4-2.

Instead of checking for `navigation.geolocation`, in this example, the geo-location-javascript API is initialized and will return whether or not the browser supports any of the geolocation APIs that geo-location-javascript does. A simpler call to `getCurrentPosition()` is made, without the timeout set, but otherwise the `getLocation()` function is very similar to this same function in Example 4-2.

Nothing changed between the two geolocation examples in the `plotLocation()` function, however there are big changes in the `reportProblem()` function. First, note that there is no *PositionError* object passed to the function—geo-location-javascript does not have this functionality. The error handling is very simplistic, and this is one of the biggest drawbacks of this API. As I said earlier, this works adequately because we are using a simple example. However, should the geolocation needs be more complex, a lot of additional coding will be needed to get the application working correctly.

An ArcGIS JavaScript API Example

Esri's ArcGIS API for JavaScript allows the developer to take advantage of all the mapping, editing, geocoding, and geoprocessing services that Esri offers. With this API, a developer is able to embed a map that functions, like those on *http://www.arcgis .com/*, and to customize its look and functionality to satisfy the needs of the application being built. The JavaScript API is hosted on ArcGIS Online and is freely available for use. Many sites use this API for their GIS needs, especially when their desktop and server GIS needs are met using Esri enterprise software. At the time of this writing, the current version of the API is 2.2.

The ArcGIS JavaScript API, Briefly

Again, for this book, I have included all of the code for the ArcGIS JavaScript Map application into a single HTML file to make it easier to read. In a production application, I would break the CSS and JavaScript into their own files.

Take a look at the code in Example 4-4, which contains everything needed to create a simple ArcGIS JavaScript Map application.

Example 4-4. A simple Esri ArcGIS Map

```
<!DOCTYPE html>
<html>
  <head>
    <meta charset="utf-8">
    <meta http-equiv="X-UA-Compatible" content="IE=7"/>
    <meta http-equiv="viewport"
        content="initial-scale=1, maximum-scale=1, user-scalable=no"/>

    <title>A Simple Esri ArcGIS Map</title>

    <link rel="stylesheet" href="http://serverapi.arcgisonline.com/jsapi/arcgis/ \
        2.2/js/dojo/dijit/themes/claro/claro.css"/>
    <style type="text/css">
      html, body {
        height: 100%;
        margin: 0;
        padding: 0;
        width: 100%;
      }

      #map {
        height: 100%;
        width: 100%;
      }
    </style>

    <script type="text/javascript">
      var djConfig = { parseOnLoad: true };
    </script>
    <script type="text/javascript"
        src="http://serverapi.arcgisonline.com/jsapi/arcgis/?v=2.2">
    </script>
    <script type="text/javascript">
      dojo.require('esri.map');

      var map;
      var initialExtent = {
```

```
      xmin: -119.3324,
      ymin: 26.3156,
      xmax: -72.3568,
      ymax: 55.0558,
      /*
       * Web Mercator (102113), or WGS 84 (4326) - these are the
       * only two that support continuous pan across the date line
       */
      spatialReference: { wkid: 4326 }
    };
    var startExtent;
    var basemap;

    function initApp() {
      var startExtent = new esri.geometry.Extent(initialExtent);

      map = new esri.Map('map', {
        extent: startExtent,
        wrapAround180: true
      });

      basemap = new esri.layers.ArcGISTiledMapServiceLayer(
          'http://server.arcgisonline.com/ArcGIS/rest/services/' +
          'ESRI_StreetMap_World_2D/MapServer');
      map.addLayer(basemap);
    }

    dojo.addOnLoad(initApp);
  </script>
</head>
<body class="claro">
  <div id="map"></div>
</body>
</html>
```

The code in Example 4-4 produces a map like that shown in Figure 4-2. I will step through this code in more detail in a moment, but there are several things that should be noted right away:

- The application is written in HTML5.
- The Esri ArcGIS API for JavaScript is included in the application by calling it from ArcGIS Online.
- The Dojo Toolkit (*http://dojotoolkit.org/*), with its immense functionality, is also included in the API call to ArcGIS Online.
- An ArcGIS JavaScript Map is created by specifying the container, a `<div>` element, to hold the map, and a set of inline options that define aspects of the map being created.

As with the Google Map examples, I chose to write this application in HTML5, as it will soon be the industry standard. Plus this will give it additional functionality for creating more impressive maps in the future. Any true DOCTYPE may, of course, be used and the application will run fine.

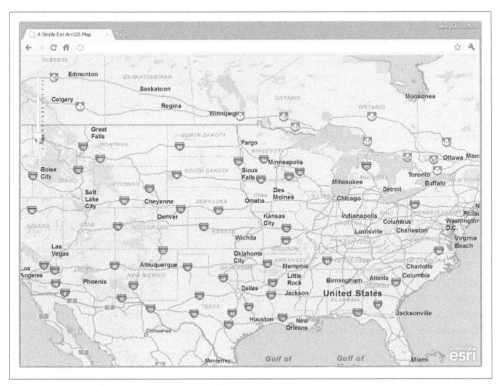

Figure 4-2. A simple Esri ArcGIS Map in Chrome

The Esri ArcGIS JavaScript API and Dojo Toolkit are included in the application with the following line:

```
<script type="text/javascript"
    src="http://serverapi.arcgisonline.com/jsapi/arcgis/?v=2.2">
</script>
```

The version of the API you wish to use is specified in the *querystring* of the API call, in this case the latest version: 2.2.

Once again, I am using a <meta> element to specify the viewport, telling it to set the application to full-screen and not allow the user to resize the application—this is an iPhone recognizable element. There is a second <meta> element, however, that is used for Internet Explorer browsers, telling them to interpret and display the application as Internet Explorer 7 would. This element should change as usage of the IE7 browser finally disappears.

A *Map* is created by instantiating a new esri.Map object and specifying the element that will contain the map. The element is referenced by its id value. The *Map* object also accepts an "options" object that controls initial extent and other map values. For example, the `wrapAround180` property, which is new to the 2.2 API, tells the map whether or not to continuously pan across the date line. In all previous versions of the JavaScript API, the map would not scroll across the date line like other web-mapping applications do.

For more information on options available for the *Map* object, or API details in general, visit the ArcGIS API for JavaScript Resource page (*http://help.arcgis.com/en/webapi/ javascript/arcgis/*).

Adding Geolocation to Esri Maps

You probably noticed the similarities between the map applications in Example 4-1 and Example 4-4 or, more specifically, the way in which a map was created with each API. While the applications themselves are fairly similar, the way geolocation is added to both of them is nearly identical. To add W3C Geolocation API code to the ArcGIS JavaScript application, we add the same basic code that we did for the Google Map.

First, we will create a function `getLocation()` to handle checking for the `navigator.geo location` object and for making the call to `getCurrentPosition()`. This function will once again take advantage of a global variable called `browserSupport` that will eventually let our *errorCallBack* function know if the error is from the API or a lack of browser support. Example 4-5 shows the geolocation functionality added to our Esri ArcGIS Map example. Changes and additions to the original code are highlighted in bold.

Example 4-5. Adding geolocation to an Esri ArcGIS Map

```
<!DOCTYPE html>
<html>
  <head>
    <meta charset="utf-8">
    <meta http-equiv="X-UA-Compatible" content="IE=7"/>
    <meta http-equiv="viewport"
        content="initial-scale=1, maximum-scale=1, user-scalable=no"/>

    <title>Adding Geolocation to an Esri ArcGIS Map</title>

    <link rel="stylesheet" href="http://serverapi.arcgisonline.com/jsapi/arcgis/ \
        2.2/js/dojo/dijit/themes/claro/claro.css"/>
    <style type="text/css">
      html, body {
        height: 100%;
        margin: 0;
        padding: 0;
        width: 100%;
      }

      #map {
        height: 100%;
        width: 100%;
      }
```

```
</style>

<script type="text/javascript">
  var djConfig = { parseOnLoad: true };
</script>
<script type="text/javascript"
    src="http://serverapi.arcgisonline.com/jsapi/arcgis/?v=2.2">
</script>
<script type="text/javascript">
  dojo.require('esri.map');

  var map;
  var initialExtent = {
      xmin: -119.3324,
      ymin: 26.3156,
      xmax: -72.3568,
      ymax: 55.0558,
      /*
       * Web Mercator (102113), or WGS 84 (4326) - these are the
       * only two that support continuous pan across the date line
       */
      spatialReference: { wkid: 4326 }
  };
  var startExtent;
  var basemap;
  var browserSupport = false;
  var attempts = 0;

  function initApp() {
    var startExtent = new esri.geometry.Extent(initialExtent);

    map = new esri.Map('map', {
        extent: startExtent,
        wrapAround180: true
      });

    basemap = new esri.layers.ArcGISTiledMapServiceLayer(
            'http://server.arcgisonline.com/ArcGIS/rest/services/' +
            'ESRI_StreetMap_World_2D/MapServer');
    map.addLayer(basemap);

    /* Add Geolocation */
    dojo.connect(map, 'onLoad', function() {
      getLocation();
    });
  }

  /*
   * If the W3C Geolocation object is available then get the current
   * location, otherwise report the problem
   */
  function getLocation() {
    /* Check if the browser supports the W3C Geolocation API */
    if (navigator.geolocation) {
      browserSupport = true;
```

```
      navigator.geolocation.getCurrentPosition(plotLocation,
          reportProblem, { timeout: 45000 });
    } else
      reportProblem();
}

/* Plot the location on the map and zoom to it */
function plotLocation(position) {
  attempts = 0;

  var pointsLayer = new esri.layers.GraphicsLayer();

  map.addLayer(pointsLayer);

  var point = new esri.geometry.Point(position.coords.longitude,
      position.coords.latitude, new esri.SpatialReference({
        wkid: 4326
      }));
  pointsLayer.add(
    new esri.Graphic(
      point,
      new esri.symbol.SimpleMarkerSymbol().setColor(
          new dojo.Color([255, 0, 0, 0.5]))
    )
  );
  map.centerAndZoom(point, 13);
}

/* Report any errors using this function */
function reportProblem(e) {
  /* Is this a support issue or an API issue? */
  if (browserSupport) {
    switch (e.code) {
      case e.PERMISSION_DENIED:
        alert('You have denied access to your position. You will ' +
            'not get the most out of the application now.');
        break;
      case e.POSITION_UNAVAILABLE:
        alert('There was a problem getting your position.');
        break;
      case e.TIMEOUT:
        /* Three changes to get the location before a true timeout */
        if (++attempts < 3) {
          navigator.geolocation.getCurrentPosition(plotLocation,
              reportProblem);
        } else
          alert('The application has timed out attempting to get ' +
              'your location.');
          break;
      default:
        alert('There was a horrible Geolocation error that has ' +
            'not been defined.');
    }
  } else
    alert('Geolocation is not supported by your browser.');
```

```
      }
    dojo.addOnLoad(initApp);
  </script>
</head>
<body class="claro">
  <div id="map"></div>
</body>
</html>
```

In this example, the call to the `getLocation()` function is inside an anonymous function that will be called on an `onLoad` event from the *Map*. Next, we define our two callback functions: `plotLocation()` and `reportProblem()`. The `reportProblem()` function is exactly like its counterpart in Example 4-2, so there is no need to go into it again. `plotLocation()`, however, is much changed as different APIs handle adding points differently.

The `plotLocation()` function first creates an `esri.layers.GraphicsLayer` called `points Layer`, which is where the new point will be placed, and adds this layer to the map. It then creates a new `esri.geometry.Point`, `point`, with the coordinates passed from the *Position* object. Next, it adds a new graphic on the `pointsLayer` layer, at `point`, with an `esri.symbol.SimpleMarkerSymbol`. Finally, the map is centered and zoomed to the current geolocation.

Support for Other Browsers

The code in Example 4-5 will provide geolocation support for browsers that implement the W3C Geolocation API. Once again, we need to rewrite our code to utilize the geo-location-javascript library to give us cross-browser support for our geolocation application. Example 4-6 shows an implementation of a cross-browser geolocation application using geo-location-javascript within the Esri ArcGIS JavaScript API. I have again highlighted the changes in the code in bold so they are easier to see.

Example 4-6. Adding geolocation for other browsers to an Esri ArcGIS Map

```
<!DOCTYPE html>
<html>
  <head>
    <meta charset="utf-8">
    <meta http-equiv="X-UA-Compatible" content="IE=7"/>
    <meta http-equiv="viewport"
        content="initial-scale=1, maximum-scale=1, user-scalable=no"/>

    <title>Adding Geolocation for Other Browsers to an Esri Map</title>

    <link rel="stylesheet" href="http://serverapi.arcgisonline.com/jsapi/arcgis/ \
        2.2/js/dojo/dijit/themes/claro/claro.css"/>
    <style type="text/css">
      html, body {
        height: 100%;
        margin: 0;
```

```
      padding: 0;
      width: 100%;
    }

    #map {
      height: 100%;
      width: 100%;
    }
</style>

<script type="text/javascript">
  var djConfig = { parseOnLoad: true };
</script>
<script type="text/javascript"
    src="http://serverapi.arcgisonline.com/jsapi/arcgis/?v=2.2">
</script>
<script type="text/javascript" src="gears_init.js"></script>
<script type="text/javascript" src="geo.js"></script>
<script type="text/javascript">
  dojo.require('esri.map');

  var map;
  var initialExtent = {
      xmin: -119.3324,
      ymin: 26.3156,
      xmax: -72.3568,
      ymax: 55.0558,
      /*
       * Web Mercator (102113), or WGS 84 (4326) - these are the
       * only two that support continuous pan across the date line
       */
      spatialReference: { wkid: 4326 }
  };
  var startExtent;
  var basemap;
  var browserSupport = false;

  function initApp() {
    var startExtent = new esri.geometry.Extent(initialExtent);

    map = new esri.Map('map', {
        extent: startExtent,
        wrapAround180: true
      });

    basemap = new esri.layers.ArcGISTiledMapServiceLayer(
          'http://server.arcgisonline.com/ArcGIS/rest/services/' +
          'ESRI_StreetMap_World_2D/MapServer');
    map.addLayer(basemap);

    /* Add Geolocation */
    dojo.connect(map, 'onLoad', function() {
      getLocation();
    });
  }
```

```
    /*
     * The browser will now use whatever geolocation API is available to
     * it; hopefully it will be the W3C Geolocation object that is used to
     * get the current location. If there is no geolocation support at all,
     * then report the problem.
     */
    function getLocation() {
      /* Check if the browser supports any geolocation API */
      if (geo_position_js.init()) {
        browserSupport = true;
        geo_position_js.getCurrentPosition(plotLocation,
            reportProblem);
      } else
        reportProblem();
    }


    /* Plot the location on the map and zoom to it */
    function plotLocation(position) {
      attempts = 0;

      var pointsLayer = new esri.layers.GraphicsLayer();

      map.addLayer(pointsLayer);

      var point = new esri.geometry.Point(position.coords.longitude,
          position.coords.latitude, new esri.SpatialReference({
            wkid: 4326
          }));
      pointsLayer.add(
        new esri.Graphic(
          point,
          new esri.symbol.SimpleMarkerSymbol().setColor(
              new dojo.Color([255, 0, 0, 0.5]))
        )
      );
      map.centerAndZoom(point, 13);
    }

    /* Report any errors using this function */
    function reportProblem() {
      /* Is this a support issue or an API issue? */
      if (browserSupport)
        alert('Could not locate your device.');
      else
        alert('Geolocation is not supported by your browser.');
    }

    dojo.addOnLoad(initApp);
  </script>
</head>
<body class="claro">
  <div id="map"></div>
```

```
    </body>
</html>
```

Calls to `gears_init.js` and `geo.js` load the libraries we are using for geolocation in this example. The *Map* functionality itself remains the same as in Example 4-5.

Instead of checking for `navigator.geolocation`, the geo-location-javascript `init()` function is called, which returns whether or not the browser supports any geolocation API. A simpler call to `getCurrentPosition()` is made, without the timeout set, but otherwise the `getLocation()` function is very similar to this same function in Example 4-5.

Nothing changed between the two Esri geolocation examples in the `plotLocation()` function, but there are, obviously, big changes in the `reportProblem()` function because of the lack of a *PositionError* object with geo-location-javascript. This is what we saw back in Example 4-3.

For more complicated cross-browser geolocation needs, additional and more complex coding will be required to get the job done. Hopefully the geo-location-javascript library will eventually add more functionality to its code base so that it better mirrors the W3C Geolocation API methods and properties. Until that day, it is up to application developers to write this functionality themselves. It is either that, or everyone needs to stop using outdated legacy browsers and phones—but unfortunately I do not see that happening for a few years still.

## CHAPTER 5

Saving Geographic Information

Many applications do more than display a geolocation on a map once it has been acquired. In many cases, the location is saved for later use—possibly displaying a history of where a user has been, or showing where many users are at any given time. In these cases, the browser application will need to collect the geolocation of the device and then send that information to a server for further processing. Most of this backend processing is beyond the scope of this book, but most likely a web server will be used with a server-side language like PHP, Python, C# or VB.NET, Java, etc. The language used does not really matter, but how the information is saved does matter.

 For more information on server-side scripting languages, check out some of these titles to get you started: *PHP and MySQL Development, 4th Edition* by Luke Welling and Laura Thomson (Addison-Wesley Professional), *Programming Python, Fourth Edition* (*http://oreilly.com/ catalog/9780596158118/*) by Mark Lutz (O'Reilly Media), *Head First Java, Second Edition* (*http://oreilly.com/catalog/9780596009205/*) by Kathy Sierra and Bert Bates (O'Reilly Media), and *Beginning ASP.NET 4: in C# and VB* by Imar Spaanjaars (Wrox).

Since I want to concentrate more on what to do with the geographic information once it has been collected by the browser than how to manipulate it on the server, I will talk specifications more than implementation in the sections to come. There are many ways that geolocation information can be saved for later use: text files, CSV files, XML files, JSON files, KML files, Shapefiles, geodatabases, relational databases, etc. How you decide to save your geometry is going to depend on several factors, including GIS environment, operating systems, and budget.

For example, if you have a limited budget, then going a more open-source route with your GIS needs might be in order. In this case, using KML and Google Maps might be the right direction. If you are in an enterprise environment, however, then you are more likely to be using ArcGIS Desktop and other Esri products. In this type of environment, a more robust Oracle database might be in order. Knowing that there are many solutions to a problem is important knowledge that I hope you take advantage of in your own projects.

I will focus on only three of the ways data can be saved—KML, Shapefiles, and relational databases—because they are all popular ways of saving geographic information. If none of these proves to be a good method for your needs, hopefully it will at least aid you in learning how you can store your data using a different format.

KML

Keyhole Markup Language (KML) is an XML file format designed to hold geographic information that is to be visualized on Internet-based maps and browsers, such as Google Maps and Google Earth. It was originally created by Keyhole, Inc., which was purchased by Google in 2004. Google submitted the KML 2.2 specification to the Open Geospatial Consortium (OGC) (*http://www.opengeospatial.org/*) to ensure that KML remained an open standard. It became an official OGC standard on April 14, 2008.

 Often times you will see a *KMZ* file extension—this is a zipped file that contains a compressed version of one or more *KML* files and their associated icon and image files.

KML has many uses for geospatial information, one of which is holding point data—which I am sure you have figured out by now is the focus of geolocation. In KML, a point is held within a `<Placemark>` container. This container holds a *name*, *description*, and *Point* geometry, at a minimum. A *Simple Point Placemark* is shown here:

```
<?xml version="1.0" encoding="UTF-8"?>
<kml xmlns="http://www.opengis.net/kml/2.2">
  <Placemark>
    <name>Simple placemark</name>
    <description>This is an example of a simple placemark.</description>
    <Point>
      <coordinates>-90.185278,38.624722</coordinates>
    </Point>
  </Placemark>
</kml>
```

There are basically three types of *Point Placemark* that can be created:

- Simple
- Floating
- Extruded

A *Simple Point Placemark* will always be attached to the ground, meaning it will always be displayed at the height of the underlying terrain. A *Floating Point Placemark* has a specific height at which it is defined to be above the ground height. An *Extruded Point*

Placemark is similar to the *Floating Point Placemark* in that it is at a specific height above the ground, but it is tethered to the ground by a customizable tail. All three of these types are controlled by the data inside the `<Point>` element of the `<Placemark>`.

The following illustrates the syntax of a *Point Placemark*, showing the child elements that would be associated with geolocation. For a full list of the elements that can be added as children of a *Placemark*, see the KML Reference, Placemark at *http://code .google.com/apis/kml/documentation/kmlreference.html#placemark*:

```
<Placemark id="ID">
  <name>...</name>                  <!-- string -->
  <description>...</description>     <!-- string -->
  <Timestamp>
    <when>...</when>                 <!-- kml:dateTime -->
  </Timestamp>
  <ExtendedData>...</ExtendedData>   <!-- custom -->
  <Point id="ID">
    <extrude>...</extrude>           <!-- boolean -->
    <altitudeMode>...</altitudeMode>
          <!-- clampToGround, relativeToGround, or absolute -->
    <coordinates>...</coordinates>   <!-- long,lat[,alt] -->
  </Point>
</Placemark>
```

Looking at the `<Point>` element, you will see that it has three children, `<extrude>`, `<altitudeMode>`, and `<coordinates>`. The `<coordinates>` element is required by any of the three types of *Point Placemark* and contains a latitude and longitude measured in decimal degrees referenced with WGS 84, and an optional altitude measured in meters above sea level. When an `<altitudeMode>` element is added to the `<Point>` element, the *Point Placemark* becomes *Floating* or *Extruded*. Determining which of these types it is falls to whether or not the `<extrude>` element is set to *true* with a value of 1.

Example 5-1 shows a KML file with several points in it, along with all of the information that can be gathered by the W3C Geolocation API.

Example 5-1. Sample KML file with geolocation information

```
<?xml version="1.0" encoding="UTF-8"?>
<kml xmlns="http://www.opengis.net/kml/2.2">
  <Document>
    <Placemark id="pt_000000">
      <name>Point 000000</name>
      <description>This is the first point collected.</description>
      <Timestamp><when>2011-04-06T23:24:12+06:00</when></Timestamp>
      <ExtendedData>
        <Data name="accuracy"><value>20</value></Data>
        <Data name="altitudeAccuracy"><value>100</value></Data>
        <Data name="heading"><value>NaN</value></Data>
        <Data name="speed"><value>0</value></Data>
      </ExtendedData>
      <Point>
        <extrude>0</extrude>
        <altitudeMode>relativeToGround</altitudeMode>
```

```
        <coordinates>-90.185278,38.624722,212</coordinates>
      </Point>
    </Placemark>
    <Placemark id="pt_000001">
      <name>Point 000001</name>
      <description>This is the second point collected.</description>
      <Timestamp><when>2011-04-07T00:15:37+06:00</when></Timestamp>
      <ExtendedData>
        <Data name="accuracy"><value>10</value></Data>
        <Data name="altitudeAccuracy"><value>10</value></Data>
        <Data name="heading"><value>37</value></Data>
        <Data name="speed"><value>15.6464</value></Data>
      </ExtendedData>
      <Point>
        <extrude>0</extrude>
        <altitudeMode>relativeToGround</altitudeMode>
        <coordinates>-89.788221,38.4233,18</coordinates>
      </Point>
    </Placemark>
    <Placemark id="pt_000002">
      <name>Point 000002</name>
      <description>This is the third point collected.</description>
      <Timestamp><when>2011-04-07T11:49:03+06:00</when></Timestamp>
      <ExtendedData>
        <Data name="accuracy"><value>60</value></Data>
        <Data name="altitudeAccuracy"><value>80</value></Data>
        <Data name="heading"><value>147</value></Data>
        <Data name="speed"><value>31.2928</value></Data>
      </ExtendedData>
      <Point>
        <extrude>0</extrude>
        <altitudeMode>relativeToGround</altitudeMode>
        <coordinates>-90.123129,37.992331,25</coordinates>
      </Point>
    </Placemark>
  </Document>
</kml>
```

Although the latitude, longitude, altitude, and timestamp can be included natively, the rest of the geolocation information—accuracy, altitudeAccuracy, heading, and speed—needs to be added in the <ExtendedData> element and defined there for use. There are three ways this data can be added; see the KML Reference, ExtendedData at *http://code.google.com/apis/kml/documentation/kmlreference.html#extendeddata* for more information on these methods. I chose the data pair method so that the values would be shown in Google Earth, but one of the other methods might better suit your application needs.

Because KML is basically text in a file, it is a fairly straightforward bit of programming on the server-side of an application to create this file, read from it, or write to it regardless of the technology being used. Also, because of its XML nature, converting the data in the KML file to a different format is also not that difficult. Working with KML is easy and makes it a good choice for storing geolocation data.

Shapefiles

A *shapefile* is a data format designed for holding geographical vector data like points and polygons along with associated attribute data. It was developed by Esri and is maintained by it. It was specifically designed as a spatial data format for use with Esri's ArcGIS Desktop product, though it works with other software as well. Some other software that can utilize the shapefile format include AutoCAD Map (*http://usa.auto desk.com/autocad-map-3d/*), MapInfo (*http://www.pbinsight.com/welcome/mapinfo/*), GeoMedia (*http://www.intergraph.com/sgi/products/default.aspx*), and GRASS (*http://grass.fbk.eu/*).

There are tools available to convert shapefiles to other formats and vice versa, making this a flexible format for holding geolocation information. By holding the point data in a shapefile, it can easily be converted to another format when needed. Some conversion programs are SHP2KML (*http://www.zonums.com/shp2kml.html*), shp2CAD (*http://www.zonums.com/shp2cad.html*), and SHP2MIF (*http://www.starbacks.ca/~vmushin skiy/free/shp2mif.htm*). The reverse of these programs can also easily be located with a quick web search.

Though it is called a shapefile, the format is actually a set of files that work together to produce the necessary working data. There are three or more files needed for a shapefile, as shown in Table 5-1.

Table 5-1. Files associated with a shapefile[a]

Extension	Description	Required
.shp	Stores the feature geometry.	yes
.shx	Stores the index of the feature geometry.	yes
.dbf	Stores the attribute information of the feature in a dBASE table.	yes
.sbn/.sbx	Stores the spatial index of the features.	no
.fbn/.fbx	Stores the spatial index of the features that are read-only.	no
.ain/.aih	Stores the attribute index of the active fields in a table or a theme's attribute table.	no
.atx	Stores the attribute index for the dBASE table.	no
.ixs	Stores the geocoding index for read/write shapefiles.	no
.mxs	Stores the geocoding index for read/write shapefiles (ODB format).	no
.prj	Stores the coordinate system information.	no
.xml	Stores metadata for the feature.	no
.cpg	Stores the codepage for identifying the character set to be used by the shapefile.	no

[a] ArcGIS Resource Center, Desktop 10, Shapefile file extensions. *http://help.arcgis.com/en/arcgisdesktop/10.0/help/index.html#/Shapefile _file_extensions/005600000003000000/*

To be useful to a web application, there needs to be a way to programmatically manipulate a shapefile and perform all necessary operations on it (create, read/write, etc.) For instance, the Shapefile C Library (*http://shapelib.maptools.org/*) serves as a way to write C programs that give reading, writing, and some updating capabilities to a developer. A more useful scripting library for web applications is the Python Shapefile Library.

Python Shapefile Library

The Python Shapefile Library (*http://code.google.com/p/pyshp/*) (PSL) was written by Joel Lawhead. It provides read and write capabilities for shapefiles using the Python scripting language. It is designed to be as extensible as it can be when creating a shapefile while still having some validation to ensure a proper file is produced. Take a look at Example 5-2.

Example 5-2. Creating a Shapefile with the Python Shapefile Library

```
# Include the Python Shapefile Library
import shapefile as sf

# Name of the shapefile to create
filename = 'shapefiles/geolocation'

# Create a /point/ shapefile, and turn on autoBalance
sf_w = sf.Writer(sf.POINT)
sf_w.autoBalance = 1

# Add the points
sf_w.point(-90.185278, 38.624722, 212)
sf_w.point(-89.788221, 38.4233, 18)
sf_w.point(-90.123129, 37.992331, 25)

# Create attribute information
sf_w.field('Name', 'C', 20)
sf_w.field('Description', 'C', 80)
sf_w.field('Timestamp', 'D')
sf_w.field('Accuracy', 'N', 4, 0)
sf_w.field('AltitudeAccuracy', 'N', 4, 0)
sf_w.field('Heading', 'N', 9, 6)
sf_w.field('Speed', 'N', 7, 4)

# Add attribute information
sf_w.record('Point 000000', 'This is the first point collected.', \
    '2011-04-06T23:24:12+06:00', 20, 100, None, 0)
sf_w.record('Point 000001', 'This is the second point collected.', \
    '2011-04-07T00:15:37+06:00', 10, 10, 37, 15.6464)
sf_w.record('Point 000002', 'This is the third point collected.', \
    '2011-04-07T11:49:03+06:00', 60, 80, 147, 31.2928)

# Save the file
sf_w.save(filename)
```

```
# Create a projection file
prj = open("%s.prj" % filename, 'w')
epsg = 'GEOGCS["WGS 84",DATUM["WGS_1984",SPHEROID["WGS 84",6378137, \
    298.257223563]],PRIMEM["Greenwich",0],UNIT["degree", \
    0.0174532925199433]]'
prj.write(epsg)
prj.close()
```

The first line of code imports PSL into the working script. After specifying that the shapefile will be a *POINT* type using the *Writer* object, the property autoBalance is set to *true*. This verifies that when a point or a record is added with the script, the opposite is also added (every point has a record and every record has a point). Next, the points are added with the point() method. The point() method takes a latitude, longitude, and optional altitude and measure. In Example 5-2, the latitude, longitude, and altitude of each point is recorded.

Before attribute records can be added to the shapefile, the attributes must be defined using the field() method. The field() method takes a field name, field type, field length, and (for numbers) decimal length. Once defined, the records, one for each point, are created using the record() method. After the records have been added, the shapefile is saved and the three required files (*.shp*, *.shx*, and *.dbf*) are created. Additionally, Example 5-2 creates a *.prj* file for a more complete shapefile instance.

In most cases, the shapefile holding the geolocation information will already be created when the application needs to add another record. The following code shows a small script that can edit an existing shapefile and add another point to it:

```
import shapefile as sf
filename = 'shapefiles/geolocation'
sf_e = sf.Editor(shapefile = filename + '.shp')
sf_e.point(-102.125532, 34.223411, 40)
sf_e.record('Point 000004', 'This is an appended point. ', \
'2011-04-10T01:52:22+06:00', 20, 30, 118, 17.21)
sf_e.save(filename)
```

The code for editing an existing shapefile and adding a point is simple. Updating existing points is a little more complicated, however. The *Editor* object takes care of inserting and deleting records in the shapefile. The specific record number needs to be obtained by first reading the shapefile and locating the record (also something PSL can do). Then the record should be deleted using the delete() method, and a new record with the corrected information should be added to the shapefile.

The Python Shapefile Library is fairly easy to use, even if you do not know a lot of Python to start with. The only downside to this library is that it does not have the best documentation available. Otherwise, it is a great way to manipulate shapefiles within a web application.

Databases

A *database* is an organized collection of data that is built so that the data can be stored, manipulated, and retrieved in an easy manner. The typical databases used for geographic information are *relational database management systems* (RDBMS), though it is also possible to store the data in *object database management systems* (ODBMS). Note that for the rest of this chapter, when I refer to a database, I am referring to an RDBMS. Some examples of common RDBMS systems are dBASE, Microsoft SQL Server, MySQL, Oracle, PostgreSQL, and Sybase.

Spatial databases are built so that the spatial data and attributes coexist in the same database. MySQL, DB2, Oracle, and Microsoft SQL Server (starting with 2008) all can store spatial information natively in their tables. In some cases, however, additional software is placed on top of the RDBMS in order to facilitate geographic functionality (especially querying) within the database. ArcSDE, OracleSpatial, and PostGIS are examples of software that is used on top of the databases themselves to handle geographic data. OracleSpatial is built specifically for Oracle and PostGIS is built specifically for PostgreSQL, while ArcSDE works with four commercial databases. MySQL has geographic functionality built directly into it and does not require additional software.

SDE

ArcSDE (*http://www.esri.com/software/arcgis/arcsde/index.html*), or simply SDE (Spatial Database Engine), is an Esri product for storing and managing geographic data with other business data within a relational database. It is designed to run with the commercial databases IBM DB2, Informix, Microsoft SQL Server, and Oracle, as well as the open source database PostgreSQL. Starting with ArcGIS 9.2, Esri stopped selling ArcSDE as a stand-alone product and began bundling it with their ArcGIS Desktop and ArcGIS Server products. The latest release of the software at the time of this writing is 10.0. ArcSDE supports various standards, including OGC simple features, the International Organization for Standardization (ISO) spatial types, the OracleSpatial format, the PostGIS format, and the Microsoft spatial format.

PostGIS

PostGIS (*http://postgis.refractions.net/*) adds spatial functionality to the PostgreSQL relational database. It was developed by Refractions Research as an open source project and is released under the GNU General Public License. The first stable version (1.0) of the software was released in 2005. The current version of the software (as of this writing) is 1.5.2. PostGIS, which acts like ArcSDE or OracleSpatial, follows the OGC Simple Feature specification, though it has not been certified compliant by the OGC.

The following should give you some idea of PostGIS functionality using SQL:

```
SELECT loc.the_geom
FROM
```

```
geolocations loc INNER JOIN
(SELECT the_geom
FROM
 (SELECT the_geom, ST_Area(the_geom) AS area
  FROM parks) p
WHERE
 area > 10000) park ON ST_Intersects(loc.the_geom, park.the_geom)
```

This query finds all geolocations that are located within city parks with an area greater than 10,000 feet. To do this, it first pulls the parks polygons and calculates their areas using the PostGIS function ST_Area(). It then finds the parks with an area larger than 10,000 feet. Finally, it finds the geolocations located within the parks using the ST_Intersects() function. The results of this query is the geometry associated with each geolocation found within a city park with an area greater than 10,000 feet.

MySQL

MySQL (*http://www.mysql.com/*) is the world's most popular open source database, in use by some of the most heavily visited websites like Google, Wikipedia, YouTube, and Facebook. Instead of requiring additional software on top of itself, MySQL implements a subset of the OGC SQL with Geometry Types specification directly into its database. It has taken MySQL several releases since it first introduced spatial capabilities to get to the place where other spatial databases like PostGIS and OracleSpatial currently are.

The OGC naming conventions were not implemented in MySQL until version 5.6. Unfortunately, as of the time of this writing, the current generally available community release of MySQL is 5.5.11, which has differences in naming. For example, MySQL 5.6 would utilize the exact same SQL statement as the example in "PostGIS" on page 76. The MySQL 5.5 version of this code would look like the following:

```
SELECT loc.the_geom
FROM
geolocations loc INNER JOIN
(SELECT the_geom
FROM
 (SELECT the_geom, Area(the_geom) AS area
  FROM parks) p
WHERE
 area > 10000) park ON Intersects(loc.the_geom, park.the_geom)
```

As you can see, they are very similar in nature to one another, and anyone with some SQL and spatial database experience could figure out MySQL's version of things. Once MySQL 5.6 becomes generally available, MySQL will have caught up with its competitors, making it very attractive solution for spatial data management considering its popularity as a relational database.

To conclude the discussion on spatial data management with relational databases, Example 5-3 creates the structure our geolocations would need to match the examples in "KML" on page 70 or "Python Shapefile Library" on page 74.

Example 5-3. Creating a geolocation database in MySQL

```
CREATE DATABASE geolocations;

USE geolocations;

CREATE TABLE positions (
pos_id             INT            NOT NULL AUTO_INCREMENT PRIMARY KEY,
the_geom           POINT          NOT NULL,
altitude           DECIMAL(8, 2)  NOT NULL,
accuracy           DECIMAL(4, 0)  NOT NULL,
altitudeAccuracy   DECIMAL(4, 0)  NULL,
heading            DECIMAL(9, 6)  NULL,
speed              DECIMAL(7, 4)  NULL,
timestamp          DATETIME       NOT NULL,
name               VARCHAR(20)    NOT NULL,
description        VARCHAR(80)    NULL
);
```

This example creates a new database called `geolocations`, and then creates a table called `positions` that holds all of the attribute data that can be collected from the W3C Geolocation API. The SQL script to insert a new position record into our database would look like this:

```
INSERT INTO positions (
the_geom,
altitude,
accuracy,
altitudeAccuracy,
heading,
speed,
timestamp,
name,
description
) VALUES (
GeomFromText('POINT(-89.788221 38.4233)'),
18,
10,
10,
37,
15.6464,
'2011-04-07 00:15:37',
'Point 000001',
'This is the second point collected.'
);
```

This SQL statement adds a point with the OGC *Well-Known Text* (WKT) format using the `GeomFromText()` function. This SQL would be executed from a server-side script with values passed to it from the client after a location had been retrieved. The table creation and insertion would be almost the same in any relational database.

## CHAPTER 6

What You Can Do with Geolocation

There is no doubt that geolocation will continue to grow for years to come—just look at the ever-increasing trends among the popular location-based services for mobile phones to see why. While Foursquare, Gowalla, Twitter, Glympse, and all the rest continue impressive growth (and will continue to do so for quite some time), the W3C Geolocation API will also continue to open ever more doors for native browser applications in this market. Consider some of the following:

- Geolocation applications have gone from niche and novelty pieces of software to cultural and trendy "must-haves" in today's mobile world.
- Phones are becoming increasingly "smart," with more and more people switching from basic cell phones to smart devices, and the smartphone market is growing around the world and tapping into new markets.
- More smartphones equals more GPS-enabled devices to utilize geolocation technology.
- Companies now recognize the huge earnings potential with advertising on the popular location-based services, particularly as advertisements can be directed to individuals and specific locals.
- HTML5 and the W3C Geolocation API will allow for websites to add geolocation to their functionality, removing the native application-only nature geolocation software shared in the past.

Also, expect that the accuracy of a location will continue to improve with time. This will make geolocation more enticing to some, and scarier to others (those concerned with privacy, in particular). All of the existing methods for gathering a location will improve their precision, and perhaps new methods will be created that give better results from the start. Triangulation of a Cell ID will continue to improve due to the continuing additions of new and stronger cell towers (more towers means more signals from which to calculate). GPS will also continue to advance as new satellite systems are launched and due to improved cooperation amongst agencies and governments.

Finally, techniques for IP address tracking are improving as research and interest grows in geolocation.

 A computer scientist at the University of Electronic Science and Technology of China in Chengdu, Yong Wong, along with colleagues at Northwestern University in Evanston, Illinois, developed a method to identify a device using only an IP address to within 100 meters (690 meters on average). This without any information from the user!

Geolocation became a buzz-word in 2009 as social media applications took off with the introduction of Foursquare. The following year, technology writers dubbed 2010 "the year of the check-in" and the "year of geolocation." 2011 thus far has seen a continuation of this branding, as it is being referred to as "the mobile revolution." This year and the years to come will see more businesses embracing geolocation and social media applications. The mashup of several types of mobile applications (geolocation, social media, augmented reality) and the merging of a few existing ones should bring a more robust, diverse, and mature market.

Geomarketing

Geomarketing is a term that refers to marketing based specifically on geolocation. Advertisements on Facebook have been using this type of marketing, relying on IP addresses to locate the user logged into their site, and then customizing advertising based on this information. Search engines like Google and Bing do the same thing. This is a *passive* approach to geomarketing, and it has proved to be very effective. Taking an *active* approach to geomarketing, however, is proving to be the future of advertising.

Specials and Offers

Thanks to social media and geolocation, companies are taking a much more active approach to geomarketing on mobile platforms. An example of this type of geomarketing is the *Specials* available at certain locations in Foursquare. These *Specials* are sometimes even further "specialized" for an individual, giving the "mayor," the individual with the most check-ins, an exclusive deal or free perks.

Companies are beginning to realize, if they have not already, that there is a huge potential for gaining new customers with a business and advertising model similar to what the social media applications like Foursquare are currently doing. Geomarketing also creates the possibility for previously unseen customer loyalty, which increases revenue. In addition to the geomarketing potential in social media applications, there is also the rising coupon-based applications that also rely on geolocation. Groupon (*http://www.groupon.com/*)-like applications that benefit from knowing a user's location also give companies the ability to personalize the offers they make available to a customer.

Geomarketing in the future will rely more on the customer's current location, with applications that track the user's movements playing a large part in allowing companies to promote specials that pertain to certain locations. A scenario like the following will be possible: A person turns his vehicle onto a busy road lined with stores. A text message, email, or some other form of notification suddenly appears on his smartphone with specials for three stores located down the road. The technology for this type of functionality already exists.

Crowdsourcing

Crowdsourcing blends together two words, "crowd" and "outsourcing". Crowdsourcing has been defined as using the collective intelligence of a large and diverse group of people to complete tasks that would otherwise be done by an individual or small group. The Internet has greatly improved the idea of crowdsourcing as it has made it far easier to gain access to large numbers of people for collaborative efforts.

Thanks to crowdsourcing and geolocation technology, geographic information for natural disasters and conflicts from around the world is growing. Every day people are becoming geospatial analysts on the ground as events unfold. There have been examples of this with the earthquake in Haiti in 2010, the 2010 BP oil disaster, the unrest and revolutions in the Middle East in 2010 and 2011, and the earthquake in Japan in 2011. As a real-world instance of using crowdsourcing, ArcGIS Mobile projects were used for boom monitoring during the cleanup of the BP oil spill.

Companies have come to realize that utilizing crowdsourcing has benefits, including the following:

- Ideas can be explored without incurring large costs.
- A larger pool of talented people can be accessed to attack a problem.
- Customers' desires or feelings about brands and offers are discovered quickly.
- Giving customers a "voice" can induce brand loyalty.

Yelp brought the idea of crowdsourcing to social media, allowing users to leave both *Tips* and *Reviews* for any business in its database. Many of the social media applications have since implemented similar ideas. Learning more about a business before visiting it has become easier with these applications, and more importantly, customers can develop a tangible connection with the businesses they review—giving them a sense of ownership with the brand or business in the process.

Marketing departments are now using the reviews and tips submitted by users to shape their advertisements and to create specials and offers to match the crowd's input. In doing this, customers are receiving more personalized and relevant offers directly via their smartphones, reinforcing their feedback and brand loyalty.

Specialization

One of the goals of geomarketing, from a business's point of view, is to be able to deliver marketing and advertisements that are specific for a location to the customer. Web-based advertisements are using geolocation to deliver content that is relevant to a city level. The location is most likely found based upon IP address, so it makes sense to only deliver content that is granular to this level. After all, desktop computers are usually being used in work or home environments which do not move, so there is no need to deliver content more specific than city-wide advertisements.

The story is different for smartphones, which may be moving while a user is browsing the Web or accessing a social media application to check in at a business. In this case, more specialized forms of advertisements are much more likely to be effective.

The future of geomarketing should see more of this granular advertisement that relies on geolocation for producing specialized content for the user. More mobile applications like Shopkick will enter the market to give users specialized offers and content based solely on where they are when using the application. Giving users a sense of individual attention will succeed in building brand and company loyalty.

Think back to the scenario in "Specials and Offers" on page 80. Now, instead of driving, the person is walking through a mall. He has an application on his smartphone that is configured to give him messages pertaining to sports. As he reaches a buffer of 100 meters from a sporting goods store specializing in soccer equipment, he receives an alert that the store has a special offer expiring in 30 minutes especially for him—authentic Bayern München shirts with Arjen Robben's number 10, 25% off retail price. As he hurries to the store, he thinks to himself what an odd coincidence that he would get this offer when only an hour earlier he had tweeted on Robben's fine performance and hat-trick against Hamburg. Odd indeed, right? This type of application will be here in the near future.

Geosocial

Geosocial is a term that refers to social media based on geolocation. It was because of social media applications using geolocation for social interaction that location-based services became popular in the first place. This market will be one to watch in the future because of the its current popularity. Geosocial applications will continue to give businesses new ways to advertise to users on a more personal level. I expect the geosocial environment will expand itself to new opportunities and groups of people, as developers take new spins at social media applications.

Continued Growth

The social media industry has grown from a few applications that were built for specific communities in the United States to a global, multibillion dollar industry. As the social media market continues to grow, it will face challenges that it must meet and resolve before it can go truly mainstream. Once it does, it will go from a multibillion dollar industry to a multi-?? dollar industry.

The security that is implemented by the application is also very important for the users of the application. When the user passes information to the application for keeping, some questions that come to mind are: what type of storage is used to hold the data, how is this storage secured from being discovered by outside parties, what kinds of security are on the operating system of the server, is the server's operating system being patched from the latest security threats, and is Transport Layer Security (TLS) being used as the transportation protocol?

Security of private data is of utmost importance for any business dealing in sensitive user information. No one should ever give a program access to private data unless it is known to be trusted. Most businesses today understand the value of privacy, and go to great lengths to ensure that any private information is properly secured.

As for the future of social media applications, Ditto (*http://www.ditto.me/*) is one application that is forward-thinking, and appears to have what the social media genre needs to make it more practical and widely used. Ditto is a check-in social media application much like Foursquare. Where it differs from the traditional check-in application, though, is that Ditto asks your connected friends what they want to do, instead of what are you doing. In fact, Ditto's tag line is "What are you up to?"

There will be other applications that build on what Ditto is doing, just as other applications today built on what Yelp and other early social media applications have done. When social media applications can address specific needs for groups of people, they will make social media more accepted and useful. When something is useful, it obviously will be used by more people. Eventually, social media will go mainstream.

Automatic Check-in

Look for location-based services to be more hands-free in the future. The traditional check-in applications should transform from the current model of the user searching for the business she just arrived at and checking in, to a smarter, automated model. The application may track your geolocation for you, and make suggestions based on that location and the database of businesses it has built up. This type of application can use crowdsourcing to refine a business's location based upon the geolocation of volumes of users that check in to a particular place. By learning in this way, it will give better, more accurate suggestions the more frequently the application is used.

As technology improves and the accuracy of a geolocation gets better, applications will rely more on *automatic* check-ins at locations. Some applications may opt to provide a pop up on the phone to inform the user it is about to check him in at a location, possibly asking for verification. Depending on the purpose of the application, it could simply check the user in at the location without notifying him at all. Shopkick already takes advantage of the automatic check-in, and more applications will follow with time.

Two Way Street of Data

The data for a social media application flows from both the application and the user. The user provides information to the application, such as his current location and thoughts about a location (reviews and tips), etc. In return, the application may provide information like businesses in the vicinity of the user's location and other users nearby, etc. As you can see, there is a need for information sharing in order for social media application to work.

One of the biggest challenges that growing social media companies must concentrate on is the issue of a user's privacy. There are questions that must be addressed by any application in the social media market. How is a user's location information protected? How will information be shared between users of an application? What information from the application is available to the public?

There will, of course, need to be some shift in the idea of privacy by the general public, especially as geolocation is integrated more and more into our daily lives. For example, should a person's location in a public area be protected in the same way as a person's bank account information? The idea of what is public and what is private needs to be revised.

The social media industry will not continue to grow and advance without a greater influx of data from users. What makes these applications useful to people is that they can enhance their life in some way. This is only accomplished by having data about the user available to an application that makes the most of it.

The idea of privacy for people who were born before the 1990s is different than that of those born after, the latter showing a greater understanding of what social media is capable of—perhaps unconsciously, as they have been texting and tweeting for most of their lives. This generation has been raised with a different concept of privacy. The rest of us will have to catch up and learn to relax the idea of what private information is in order to develop applications that have more meaning. Geosocial applications have the ability to be more than check-in applications that let your friends know where you are. They can become an integral part of a person's social life.

Data is a two way street—it needs to flow in both directions in order for a social media application to function properly. The more data that an application is able to receive, the better an application it can be and the more useful it will be for a person's daily life. Data must be given in order to be received.

Geotagging

Geotagging is defined as adding geospatial metadata to digital media such as photographs, videos, text messages, tweets, and web pages. The geospatial information usually captured in the metadata is latitude and longitude, altitude, accuracy, and heading. Other information may also be gathered based on the type of media in question. As you can see, the geospatial information captured is basically the same information gathered by the W3C Geolocation API.

Digital Media and Geotagging

Twitter (*http://twitter.com/*) added geotagging support in the summer of 2009, though full API support was not available until November 2009. It is turned off by default in a user's profile—this creates an opt-in policy for geotagging tweets for the user. Turning on location can be done by going to the user settings, and checking the checkbox for *Tweet Location* under the *Account* tab. Twitter states that when a user turns on geotagging, it stores that location, though a user always has the option to delete their location history.

YouTube (*http://www.youtube.com/*) added geotagging support in the summer of 2007. This capability is available when a new video is uploaded to YouTube as an option after the *Broadcast Options* section of the *Video Upload* process. It is available under the *Date and Map Options* and can be added by either specifying the latitude and longitude coordinates or placing a point on the provided Google Maps map. When specifying the coordinates, they should be entered as follows:

```
geo:lat=38.624722 geo:lon=-90.185278
```

Many photo-sharing sites also support geotagging of the digital photographs that are shared on them. There are a lot of sites out there for photo-sharing: flickr, photobucket, picasa, photoworks, twitpic, snapfish, shutterfly, fotki—and there are many more. The major photo-sharing sites have realized the value of adding support for geotagging, as more and more of the photos being uploaded to them are coming from cameras that are built into smartphones with geotagging capabilities. As more cameras have built-in GPS capabilities, geotagging will become a standard feature on digital photographs.

Privacy and Geotagging

Privacy is naturally of concern to many people regarding geographic information shared with a tweet, video, or picture that will become publicly available to the entire Web. With tweets, where you were when you posted your 140-character thought is not quite as disconcerting as say, knowing where you were when you took the picture of the inside of your house. There are valid concerns for the privacy of information contained in videos or images especially. Proper security on public sites so that media content marked as private remains so is extremely important.

At some point, though, users will have to ask themselves whether they trust the providers to properly handle and secure their content. If the answer to that question is *no*, then these users should opt-out of geotagging their tweets and videos, and remove geographic information from photos that are uploaded to public sites. Media sites provide services, and it is up to the user to decide how much of the service they wish to utilize and be a part of.

Geo-applications

Geo-applications are applications that are built with one of their features relying on geolocation. The social media applications that I have been discussing are one example of geo-applications. There are many other applications that utilize geolocation. A great example is the CitySourced (*http://www.citysourced.com/*) application, a program designed to foster civic responsibility and participation by allowing people to report issues like potholes in streets, graffiti, and trash. There will be a greater number of these applications that utilize geolocation as we move forward with technology for everyday life.

Safety/Tracking

One of the areas that will use geolocation in applications in the future is safety, especially the safety of children and young adults. There are programs now that can track where your child is at all times by the child carrying a GPS device which broadcasts her location. The parent then uses a program to monitor the child's GPS location to make sure she is where she is supposed to be. Futuristic scenarios would allow for the child to carry a tiny device (maybe sewn into her clothing or subcutaneously injected into her skin).

There are other practical uses for this type of tracking technology. Hikers and skiers could have clothing with built in GPS transmitters. The benefit of this is obvious should they get lost or trapped in avalanches or other natural disasters. Then there is the reality of tracking troops in combat. A subcutaneous GPS device would allow for armed forces to track their soldiers in case they are captured or lost behind enemy lines. These types of devices could greatly aid in rescue efforts in both civilian and military capacities.

Taxi Services

Another good application for geolocation technology is trying to get a ride while out on the town—OK, or just getting a taxi anywhere. If you could send your geolocation to the taxi service, it could send its nearest available vehicle (because it is using GPS to track them), saving you wait time. This would not just have to be taxi services, though. The San Fransisco based start-up Uber connects people with limo drivers using an Android or iPhone application, finding the closest driver based on the user's location. Services like this will be more commonplace in the future.

Search

Searching can become more personalized if it is supplemented with geolocation. This can work with desktop computers as well, as it is not specific to smartphones. When a user searches for something, when relevant, the search engine could take into account the user's geolocation and return search results factoring in location. This could give users the result they are looking for more quickly than if the results had used a traditional weighting system. For example, you browse to the latest search engine, *Geo-Find*, and type in `family owned restaurant`. The search engine returns the results of your search with all of the family owned restaurants in your area listed first. In a normal search engine, you might get a Wikipedia entry for "family owned restaurants" first, followed by other results you do not care about before an actual family owned restaurant comes up in the results, and it is not even a restaurant located in the same state as you. Searching will change when geolocation is added as a parameter.

M-Commerce

Mobile commerce, also known as m-commerce, is the capability of doing commercial transactions using a mobile device such as a smartphone. Applications like Shopkick are already attempting to mash together geolocation and m-commerce. In time, there will be more mobile applications that take advantage of geolocation to allow consumers to make purchases based on where they are.

Other Applications

Other applications will also begin using geolocation in their functionality. It can be used as an accessory to navigation with trip tracking. It can be used as a location planning tool in conjunction with social media. Tools could be built to aid in fitness, such as by tracking your workout. If you can think of a use for geolocation, an application can be built supplement that use. The future will be filled with geolocation applications.

HTML5 and Geolocation

The future of HTML5 and the W3C Geolocation API is bright. Native geolocation applications are becoming more popular, and there are no signs of this trend changing—this is a good indication for web-based geolocation applications, as well. HTML5 is also becoming more popular, as its adoption is assured by all of the major browser makers, clearing the way for developers to create HTML5 content. Combining HTML5's abilities for better browser applications with the W3C Geolocation API will allow developers to create browser applications that rival native applications.

Web Applications Supplementing LBS

A good use of HTML5 is in supplementing mobile geolocation applications. Take Twitter, for example. It is possible to view a feed of all recent tweets within a certain buffer range of a specific coordinate. You could pick a coordinate by clicking on a map, and then displaying all tweets within 500 meters of that locations. Better yet, you could use the W3C Geolocation API to retrieve all tweets within 500 meters of your own location, as shown in Figure 6-1. Example 6-1 shows you an example.

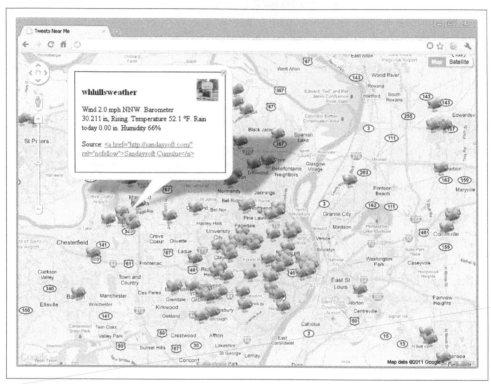

Figure 6-1. The W3C Geolocation API and Twitter Search API together

Example 6-1. An application using the Twitter Search API with geolocation

```
<!DOCTYPE html>
<html lang="en">
  <head>
    <meta charset="utf-8"/>
    <meta http-equiv="X-UA-Compatible" content="IE=7"/>
    <meta http-equiv="viewport" content="initial-scale=1, maximum-scale=1,
      user-scalable=no"/>

    <title>Tweets Near Me</title>

    <style type="text/css">
```

```
    html { height: 100% }
    body { height: 100%; margin: 0; padding: 0 }
    #map { height: 100% }
    .tweet_info { border: 1px solid #000; padding: 15px; width: 300px }
    .tweet_info img { float: right; height: 48px; margin: 0 0 10px 10px;
        width: 48px }
    .tweet_info h3 { margin-bottom: 10px }
</style>

<script type="text/javascript"
    src="http://maps.google.com/maps/api/js?sensor=true"></script>
<script type="text/javascript"
    src="https://ajax.googleapis.com/ajax/libs/jquery/1.5.2/jquery.min.js">
</script>
<script type="text/javascript" src="jquery.timer.js"></script>
<script type="text/javascript">
  var map = null;
  var browserSupport = false;
  var attempts = 0;
  var tweets = [];
  var tweetsQ = [];
  var refreshQuery = '?q=';
  var infoWindow = new google.maps.InfoWindow();

  /* This is called once the page has loaded */
  function initMap() {
    /* Set all of the options for the map */
    var options = {
      zoom: 4,
      center: new google.maps.LatLng(38.6201, -90.2003),
      mapTypeId: google.maps.MapTypeId.ROADMAP
    };

    /* Create a new Map for the application */
    map = new google.maps.Map(document.getElementById('map'), options);

    /* Set up timers to collect tweets */
    $(document).everyTime('30s', acquireTweets);
    $(document).everyTime('100ms', parseTweetsQ);

    /* Add Geolocation */
    getLocation();
  }

  /*
   * If the W3C Geolocation object is available then get the current
   * location, otherwise report the problem
   */
  function getLocation() {
    /* Check if the browser supports the W3C Geolocation API */
    if (navigator.geolocation) {
      browserSupport = true;
      navigator.geolocation.getCurrentPosition(function(position) {
          plotLocation(new google.maps.LatLng(position.coords.latitude,
              position.coords.longitude));
```

```
    }, reportProblem, { timeout: 45000 });
  } else
    reportProblem();
}

/* Create the URL that will call the Search API REST end point */
function createTweetSearchURL() {
  var temp = map.getCenter();

  return 'http://search.twitter.com/search.json' + refreshQuery +
      '&geocode=' + temp.lat() + '%2C' + temp.lng() +
      '%2C50km&rpp=100&callback=?';
}

/* Plot the location on the map and zoom to it, then get tweets */
function plotLocation(latLng) {
  attempts = 0;

  map.setCenter(latLng);
  map.setZoom(11);

  var marker = new google.maps.Marker({
    position: latLng,
    icon: 'http://geo.holdener.com/images/myloc.png',
    animation: google.maps.Animation.DROP
  });
  marker.setMap(map);

  acquireTweets();
}

/*
 * Call the Twitter Search API and cycle through results, pushing tweets
 * into the tweets queue
 */
function acquireTweets() {
  $.getJSON(createTweetSearchURL(), function(data) {
    if (data.results)
      $.each(data.results, function(i, tweet) {
        if (tweet.geo || tweet.location)
          tweetsQ.push(tweet);
      });
    refreshQuery = data.refresh_url;
  });
}

/* Parse through the queue and plot any tweets that have coordinates */
function parseTweetsQ() {
  if (tweetsQ.length > 0) {
    var tweet = tweetsQ.pop();

    /* Check to see if there are coordinates */
    if (tweet.geo) {
      tweet.latlng = new google.maps.LatLng(tweet.geo.coordinates[0],
          tweet.geo.coordinates[1]);
```

```
        plotTweet(tweet);
    }
  }
}

/* Create the content for the information pop up window */
function createInfoContent(tweet) {
  var retval = '';

  retval += '<div class="tweet_info">';
  retval += '<img alt="' + tweet.from_user_id + '" src="' +
      tweet.profile_image_url + '" class="tweet_profile"/>';
  retval += '<h3>' + tweet.from_user + '</h3>';
  retval += '<p>' + tweet.text + '</p>';
  retval += '<p>Source: <a href="' + tweet.source + '"/>' +
      tweet.source + '</a></p>';
  retval += '</div>';
  return retval;
}

/*
 * Plot the tweet on the map, and add the /click/ event to show
 * the /infoWindow/
 */
function plotTweet(tweet) {
  tweet.marker = new google.maps.Marker({
    position: tweet.latlng,
    icon: 'http://geo.holdener.com/images/tweet.png',
    animation: google.maps.Animation.DROP,
    title: tweet.from_user,
    html: createInfoContent(tweet)
  });
  google.maps.event.addListener(tweet.marker, 'click', function() {
    infoWindow.setContent(this.html);
    infoWindow.open(map, this);
  });
  tweet.marker.setMap(map);
  /*
   * If there are more than 100 tweets on the map, remove the oldest
   * one from the map
   */
  if (tweets.length > 100) {
    var tweet = tweets.shift();

    tweet.marker.setMap(null);
  }
}

/* Report any errors using this function */
function reportProblem(e) {
  /* Is this a support issue or an API issue? */
  if (browserSupport) {
    switch (e.code) {
      case e.PERMISSION_DENIED:
        alert('You have denied access to your position. You will ' +
```

```
              'not get the most out of the application now.');
          break;
      case e.POSITION_UNAVAILABLE:
          alert('There was a problem getting your position.');
          break;
      case e.TIMEOUT:
          /* Three changes to get the location before a true timeout */
          if (++attempts < 3) {
              navigator.geolocation.getCurrentPosition(plotLocation,
                  reportProblem);
          } else
              alert('The application has timed out attempting to get ' +
                  'your location.');
          break;
      default:
          alert('There was a horrible Geolocation error that has ' +
              'not been defined.');
      }
    } else
      alert('Geolocation is not supported by your browser.');
  }

  $(document).ready(initMap);
  </script>
 </head>
 <body>
   <div id="map"></div>
 </body>
</html>
```

The code starts like the Google Maps examples in Chapter 4, though there are three new style rules that will be used by the application to style an information window. After loading the Google API, the latest jQuery core library is loaded from the Google *Content Delivery Network* (CDN). After that, the jQuery Timers plugin is loaded from a local file.

Once the page has loaded, the application creates a Google Maps map with mostly default options. Afterwards, the acquireTweets() function is set to be called every 30 seconds, while the parseTweetsQ() function is set to be called every 100 milliseconds. The W3C Geolocation API is used like in the other examples.

When a successful location has been retrieved by the API, the map is centered and zoomed on those coordinates and a marker is created with a custom image and a google.maps.Animation.DROP animation. Then acquireTweets() is called manually for the first time.

acquireTweets() uses the jQuery $.getJSON() method to call the Twitter Search API. The function passes the API the latitude and longitude from the W3C Geolocation API through the geocode parameter, with a range of 50 kilometers. 100 results are returned by the call—this is set by the rpp (results per page) parameter. The resulting tweets are put into the tweetsQ array which acts as a queue of tweets to be processed. All of the options available to pass to the Search API can be found on the Twitter Search API (*http://dev.twitter.com/doc/get/search*).

A JSON object is returned by the Twitter Search API. The JSON object is structured like the following:

```
{
  "results": [
    {
      "from_user_id_str" : "111111111",
      "location": "St. Louis, MO",
      "profile_image_url":
          "http://a1.twimg.com/profile_images/111111111/my_profile_pic.gif",
      "created_at": "Wed, 20 Apr 2011 16:11:05 +0000",
      "from_user": "geotagged01",
      "id_str": "99999999999999901",
      "metadata": {
        "result_type": "recent"
      },
      "to_user_id": 222222222,
      "text": "@geotagged02 Tweet for HTML5 #Geolocation",
      "id": 99999999999999901,
      "from_user_id": 111111111,
      "to_user": "geotagged02",
      "geo": null,
      "iso_language_code": "en",
      "to_user_id_str": "222222222",
      "source": "&lt;a href=&quot;http://twitter.com/&quot;&gt;web&lt;/a&gt;"
    },
    .
    .
    .
    {
      "from_user_id_str": "222222222",
      "location": "STL",
      "profile_image_url":
          "http://a1.twimg.com/profile_images/222222222/my_profile_pic.jpg",
      "created_at": "Wed, 20 Apr 2011 16:11:05 +0000",
      "from_user": "geotagged02",
      "id_str": "99999999999999902",
      "metadata":{
        "result_type": "recent"
      },
      "to_user_id": 333333333,
      "text": "@geotagged03 Another HTML5 #Geolocation tweet",
      "id": 99999999999999902,
      "from_user_id": 222222222,
      "to_user": "geotagged03",
      "geo": null,
      "iso_language_code": "en",
      "to_user_id_str": "333333333",
      "source": "&lt;a href=&quot;http://twitter.com/&quot;&gt;Twitter \
          for Android&lt;/a&gt;"
    }
  ],
```

```
    "max_id": 99999999999999909,
    "since_id": 99999999999999902,
    "refresh_url": "?since_id=99999999999999909&q=",
    "next_page": "?page=2&max_id=99999999999999909&rpp=100&geocode=38.111111%2C \
        -90.555555%2C50.0km&q=",
    "results_per_page": 100,
    "page": 1,
    "completed_in": 0.162742,
    "warning": "adjusted since_id to 99999999999999902 (), requested since_id \
        was older than allowed -- since_id removed for pagination.",
    "since_id_str": "99999999999999902",
    "max_id_str": "99999999999999909",
    "query": ""
}
```

The `acquireTweets()` function loops through the `data.results` array and pushes every tweet that has been geotagged or has a location set by the user into the `tweetsQ` queue.

The tweets are parsed by the `parseTweetsQ` function, which, remember, is called every 100 milliseconds and pulls tweets off the tweets queue one at a time. It checks to see if this tweet has been geocoded, and if it has, it sends it to be plotted on the map. The `plotTweet()` places a custom image as a marker where the tweet originated based on its coordinates. When clicked, information about the tweet is displaying. If there are ever more than 100 tweets on the map at one time, the oldest of them is removed.

The `reportProblem()` function is the same as in other Google Maps examples, reporting problems when the Geolocation API cannot retrieve a location. The Twitter API Documentation (*http://apiwiki.twitter.com/w/page/22554679/Twitter-API-Documentation*) will give you more information on how you can leverage Twitter in a mashup that is more useful than simply streaming data back at a user.

More examples of what can be done with web applications as supplements to mobile applications are the projects dealing with Foursquare. Where Do You Go (*http://www.wheredoyougo.net/*) provides a heat map showing everywhere you go and 4mapper (*http://4mapper.appspot.com/*) does something similar, as does weeplaces (*http://www.weeplaces.com/*), though it adds a very useful timeline showing when check-ins occurred in conjunction with a map. Fourwhere (*http://www.fourwhere.com/*) combines searching through Foursquare, Yelp, and Gowalla, and displays locations on a map based on a buffer around a coordinate selected by clicking on the map.

Visualizing data is sometimes much easier for people who are wanting to digest a lot of information, especially when that data lends itself so well to being displayed on a map. HTML5 can also be used to display information in charts for another type of visualization of data. Overall, HTML5 web applications work well as a complement to their mobile counterparts. I expect to see more of these types of web applications in the future.

Web-Based LBS

Of all of the mobile applications that have been discussed in this book, there is no reason why most of them could not be written as web applications now that the W3C Geolocation API is available. Augmented reality is not really possible yet in a browser with JavaScript, but there is no reason why a social media application like Foursquare could not be written as a web application. It would serve no purpose to reinvent these existing applications as a web application version of themselves, but the development of new geolocation applications could most certainly be built for the browser.

Building for the web browser serves several purposes. Overall development costs should be lower since it can be programmed with only one code base (HTML, CSS, JavaScript, and a server-side scripting language) instead of a different code base for each platform that you wish it to run on. The client will not need special configurations, since the web application will run in the browser. Any updates are made in one place on the server and are automatically present when the user next loads the page in the browser. This means that the web application is always up-to-date.

There is also the possibility that in the future the browser will be the operating system of the device you are using, and everything done on the device will be through that browser. If this is the case, then you have positioned yourself well by creating your geolocation applications for the web browser. The W3C Geolocation API is still very new and it will take time, but more location-based services will be built for the browser. We can expect innovative geolocation applications utilizing HTML5 and the W3C Geolocation API in the future. Geolocation is here to stay.

Get even more for your money.

Join the O'Reilly Community, and register the O'Reilly books you own. It's free, and you'll get:

- $4.99 ebook upgrade offer
- 40% upgrade offer on O'Reilly print books
- Membership discounts on books and events
- Free lifetime updates to ebooks and videos
- Multiple ebook formats, DRM FREE
- Participation in the O'Reilly community
- Newsletters
- Account management
- 100% Satisfaction Guarantee

Signing up is easy:

1. **Go to: oreilly.com/go/register**
2. **Create an O'Reilly login.**
3. **Provide your address.**
4. **Register your books.**

Note: English-language books only

To order books online:
oreilly.com/store

For questions about products or an order:
orders@oreilly.com

To sign up to get topic-specific email announcements and/or news about upcoming books, conferences, special offers, and new technologies:
elists@oreilly.com

For technical questions about book content:
booktech@oreilly.com

To submit new book proposals to our editors:
proposals@oreilly.com

O'Reilly books are available in multiple DRM-free ebook formats. For more information:
oreilly.com/ebooks

Spreading the knowledge of innovators   oreilly.com

The information you need, when and where you need it.

With Safari Books Online, you can:

Access the contents of thousands of technology and business books

- Quickly search over 7000 books and certification guides
- Download whole books or chapters in PDF format, at no extra cost, to print or read on the go
- Copy and paste code
- Save up to 35% on O'Reilly print books
- **New!** Access mobile-friendly books directly from cell phones and mobile devices

Stay up-to-date on emerging topics before the books are published

- Get on-demand access to evolving manuscripts.
- Interact directly with authors of upcoming books

Explore thousands of hours of video on technology and design topics

- Learn from expert video tutorials
- Watch and replay recorded conference sessions

Spreading the knowledge of innovators   safari.oreilly.com

Milton Keynes UK
Ingram Content Group UK Ltd.
UKHW031816130923
428619UK00007B/232

9 781449 304720